D0199984

African Arguments

African Arguments is a series of short books about Africa today. Aimed at the growing number of students and general readers who want to know more about the continent, these books highlight many of the longer-term strategic as well as immediate political issues confronting the African continent. They will get to the heart of why Africa is the way it is and how it is changing. The books are scholarly but engaged, substantive as well as topical.

Series editors

Titles already published

Forthcoming

Published by Zed Books and the IAI with the support of the following organizations:

InterAfrica Group The InterAfrica Group is the regional centre for dialogue on issues of development, democracy, conflict resolution and humanitarianism in the Horn of Africa. It was founded in 1988 and is based in Addis Ababa, and has programmes supporting democracy in Ethiopia and partnership with the African Union and IGAD. <www.sas.upenn.edu/African_Studies/ Hornet/menu_Intr_Afr.html>

International African Institute The International African Institute's principal aim is to promote scholarly understanding of Africa, notably its changing societies, cultures and languages. Founded in 1926 and based in London, it supports a range of seminars and publications including the journal *Africa*. <www.internationalafricaninstitute.org>

Justice Africa Justice Africa initiates and supports African civil society activities in support of peace, justice and democracy in Africa. Founded in 1999, it has a range of activities relating to peace in the Horn of Africa, HIV/AIDS and democracy, and the African Union. <www.justiceafrica.org>

Royal African Society Now more than a hundred years old, the Royal African Society today is Britain's leading organization promoting Africa's cause. Through its journal, *African Affairs*, and by organizing meetings, discussions and other activities, the society strengthens links between Africa and Britain and encourages understanding of Africa and its relations with the rest of the world. <www.royalafricansociety.org>

Social Science Research Council The Social Science Research Council brings much-needed expert knowledge to public issues. Founded in 1923 and based in New York, it brings together researchers, practitioners and policy-makers in every continent. <www.ssrc.org>

About the author

Bronwen Manby works with the Africa Governance Monitoring and Advocacy Project (AfriMAP), an initiative of the Open Society Institute network's four African foundations established to monitor and strengthen compliance with the African Union's commitments on good governance and human rights. She was previously the deputy director of the Africa division of Human Rights Watch, and has also worked for human rights organizations in South Africa. She has written on a wide range of human rights issues in Africa, focusing especially on South Africa and Nigeria, and on continental legal developments.

BRONWEN MANBY

Struggles for citizenship in Africa

Zed Books
LONDON | NEW YORK

in association with

International African Institute
Royal African Society
Social Science Research Council

Struggles for citizenship in Africa was first published in association
with the International African Institute, the Royal African Society
and the Social Science Research Council in 2009 by Zed Books Ltd,
7 Cynthia Street, London N1 9JF, UK and Room 400, 175 Fifth Avenue,
New York, NY 10010, USA

www.zedbooks.co.uk
www.internationalafricaninstitute.org
www.royalafricansociety.org
www.ssrc.org

Cover designed by Rogue Four Design
Set in OurType Arnhem and Futura Bold by Ewan Smith, London
Index: <ed.emery@thefreeuniversity.net>
Printed and bound in Great Britain by CPI Antony Rowe, Chippenham
and Eastbourne

Distributed in the USA exclusively by Palgrave Macmillan, a division
of St Martin's Press, LLC, 175 Fifth Avenue, New York, NY 10010, USA.

A catalogue record for this book is available from the British Library
US CIP data are available from the Library of Congress
ISBN   978 1 84813 351 8 hb
ISBN   978 1 84813 352 5 pb
ISBN   978 1 84813 353 2 eb

Contents

Acknowledgements

This book is a more than usually collaborative project. Its origins lie in a project on discrimination and citizenship in Africa undertaken by the Open Society Justice Initiative, a project of the Open Society Institute, of whose British foundation I am an employee. The Justice Initiative conceived the idea of a continent-wide 'Africa citizenship audit' focusing on the use and abuse of Africa's citizenship laws for political purposes, and on the discrimination and injustice that results. The country studies included in this book are based in part on the national research carried out for the Africa citizenship audit to survey the law and practice on equality, minority rights, nationality, refugees and treatment of migrants in fourteen African countries.

I should particularly like to acknowledge the intellectual guidance and support provided by my two colleagues in the Open Society Justice Initiative, Chidi Odinkalu and Julia Harrington. Other members of the Justice Initiative team who made important contributions are Angela Khaminwa, who managed the project during its first two years, Adam Hussein, who has taken over the advocacy work, and Sebastian Köhn, who provided research assistance as well as painstaking and detailed support to the fact-checking process. Additional research assistance was provided at different times by Lisa Fuchs, Siobhan McKenna, Jonas Pohlmann, Catherine Roden and Kasia Romanska.

I should like to thank Mirna Adjami, Chaloka Beyani, Ibrahima Doumbia, Richard Dowden, Khadija Elmadmad, Alison Des Forges, Eric Goldstein, Daniel Hammett, Khoti Kamanga, Pascal Kambale, Ibrahima Kane, Gugulethu

Moyo, Mary Rayner, Dustin Sharp, Abdul Tejan Cole, Anneke van Woudenberg and Marcel Wetsh'okonda Koso for their inputs on various sections of the report.

The country research for the Africa citizenship audit was carried out by the following organizations and individuals: Ditshwanelo, Botswana; Ibrahima Doumbia, Côte d'Ivoire; Marcel Wetsh'okonda Koso (Campagne pour les Droits de l'Homme au Congo), Democratic Republic of Congo; Wesal Afifi, Abduallah Khalil, Tarek Badawy and Amal Abdel Hadi (Forced Migration and Refugee Studies Program, American University in Cairo), Egypt; Abebe Haliu, Ethiopia; Rose Ayugi, Kenya; Keiso Matashane-Marite and Libakiso Mathlo (Women and Law in Southern Africa), Lesotho; Moustapha Touré and A. S. Bouhoubeyni, Mauritania; Khadija Elmadmad, Morocco; Ilguilas Weila (Timidria), Niger; Jamesina King (Campaign for Good Governance), Sierra Leone; Karla Saller, South Africa; Sizakele Hlatshwayo (Coordinating Assembly of NGOs, CANGO), Swaziland; Lillian Keene (Mugerwa), Uganda; Patrick Matibini, Zambia; and Arnold Tsunga and Irene Petras (Zimbabwe Lawyers for Human Rights), Zimbabwe. Not all of the country cases are represented in this text, and much information collected is not included, but all informed the analysis on which it is based.

As part of this work, citizenship laws were also collected from most of Africa's countries, and a separate publication by the Open Society Institute, *Citizenship Law in Africa: A Comparative Study* (2009), provides detailed analysis of these laws. A key conclusion of the audit research and consultations was the necessity for clarification and strengthening of African norms on citizenship, and for national citizenship laws to be brought into line with human rights standards.

In memory of
Alison Des Forges,
1942–2009
and
Tajudeen Abdul-Raheem,
1956–2009

1 | Introduction

'We needed a war because we needed our identity cards. Without an identity card you are nothing in this country.' A fighter for the rebel 'new forces' in Côte d'Ivoire condensed the argument of this book into two short sentences: that the denial of a right to citizenship has been at the heart of many of the conflicts of post-colonial Africa, and that it is time to change the rules. Côte d'Ivoire may be an extreme case, but political crises since independence in the Democratic Republic of Congo, Zimbabwe, Mauritania, Uganda and elsewhere show the same pattern: political leaders seek to buttress their support among one part of their country's population by excluding another from the right to belong to the country at all.

Hundreds of thousands of people living in Africa find themselves non-persons in the only state they have ever known. They cannot get their children registered at birth or entered in school or university; they cannot access state health services; they cannot obtain travel documents, or employment without a work permit; and if they leave the country they may not be able to return. Most of all, they cannot vote, stand for office or work for state institutions.

Ultimately such policies can lead to economic and political disaster, or even war. Even where they do not, they have been used to subvert the democratic process and reinforce or prolong the hold on power of one group at the expense of another. At the expense, too, of national stability and economic progress. The result has been the mass suffering of people whose only fault may be to have the wrong last name.

Alternatively, questions of citizenship have been used to prevent specific individuals from challenging for political position or to silence those who criticize the government. At one time it seemed as though half the most important opposition politicians in Africa were allegedly not citizens of the country where they lived and worked – allegations often based on absurd arguments about ancestral origins on the wrong side of colonial borders that did not exist at the time of the individual's or his parents' birth. Kenneth Kaunda of Zambia and Alassane Ouattara of Côte d'Ivoire – a former president and a former prime minister – are only the most high-profile politicians or critics who have found themselves excluded from office or denied citizenship in this way.

Common to all these situations is the manipulation of citizenship laws: the detailed rules and regulations by which individuals can obtain recognition of their right to belong to a state, to claim equal protection under its laws, to vote in its elections and stand for office. Much as discrimination in these cases is always multifaceted, with raw violence at its extremes, the apparently dry detail of the rules for obtaining papers can hide an ocean of discrimination and denial of rights. The use and abuse of the law frames and enables the politics of ethnic exclusion. Reform of the law can be the first step back from conflict and the start of a politics of inclusion.

The pattern of these crises of citizenship is not haphazard. They are closely linked to the colonial heritage of each country; and in particular the migration and land expropriation that was implemented or facilitated by the colonial authorities. It is not a coincidence that the countries where citizenship has been most contentious are often the countries that saw the greatest colonial-era migration; migration not only of Europeans and Asians to the continent, but in even greater numbers of Africans within the continent.

Today, however, the children, grandchildren and great-grandchildren of those who migrated are now regarded as foreigners without a true claim to belong to the new polity. Yet they are in the land of their birth and lifelong residence and have no claim on the protection of any other state. Millions of people are thus presumed to have the right to exercise citizenship rights, including the right to vote or stand for office or be appointed an official, only in some other country that they have never seen. Politically disenfranchised, there is no demonstration of loyalty that can satisfy the requirements of the law.

This injustice is multiplied by a gender inequality in the law which still in many countries disallows women who marry non-citizens from passing their own citizenship to their children or their husband, though men can do so without question. The victims of this sort of discrimination are mostly invisible in the media, because they are dispersed throughout wider populations, yet those affected must number in the millions across the continent.

Citizenship law in Africa: a history of discrimination and exclusion

Africa's 'artificial' borders are often blamed for Africa's wars. The borders of all the African states, even those that were not themselves colonized, were set by European colonial powers; most of them during the notorious Berlin conference of 1884–85 that marked the end of the 'Scramble for Africa'. In 1964 the Organization of African Unity (OAU), the club of Africa's newly independent states, decided to stick with these borders and not renegotiate them. There has been much discussion about the wisdom of this decision, and whether the leaders of the newly independent countries should rather have aimed to redesign African borders along more 'natural' lines: that is, along lines that followed boundaries of language and ethnicity and pre-colonial political structures, rather than being set with ruler and map by people thousands of miles away who had never seen the land they were dividing up.

Borders throughout the world have been established by war and conquest, and Africa is unusual rather in the abruptness of the transition than in the arbitrariness of the outcome. Yet the rapidity both of the creation of African colonies and of the winning of independence from the late 1950s at the end of less than a century of European rule meant that the leaders who took control of Africa's new states faced a particular challenge to create an 'imagined community'[1] among groups of people thrown together without their own permission. The colonial period was both long enough to do very serious damage to pre-existing institutions of government, and too short to create strong new institutions that had more than the most superficial legitimacy in the eyes of the populace. Africa's post-colonial history shows how difficult it has been to create a functioning polity from scratch among peoples without a history of common political organization; but also how surprisingly persistent is the attachment to the units created by the colonizers.

In addition to bequeathing an inherent institutional weakness to the new states, the European empires also left a legacy of legal systems that had created a many-tiered citizenship structure whose central feature was racial discrimination. The colonies were founded on a basis of racial and ethnic distinction that justified the gaps in standard of living and legal rights between rulers and ruled. On the one hand there were European settlers – who were full citizens with the same rights as their relatives who lived in the 'home' country of the colonizers; and on the other there were African 'natives' (*indigènes*) – who were subjects.[2] With the exception of a small minority admitted to full citizenship, the native or *indigène* was a subordinate being without full rights, and regarded as essentially a child under European guardianship. Those from other continents (especially Asia) or of mixed race occupied a middle position often with their own specific rules. Throughout Africa, racial discrimination determined not only political rights, but also freedom of movement, and most importantly the right to hold land. In the 'settler colonies' deemed suitable for large-scale white immigration the distinctions were particularly marked, but throughout Africa whites were eligible for freehold title to land granted by the colonial state; Africans' rights to hold land were often both geographically restricted and conceptually limited to what the colonial power interpreted their subjects' 'traditional' laws to be.

At the same time, paradoxically, the law often favoured those

4

Africans who were believed to be 'native' to a place over those other Africans who had migrated there more recently – including those who had moved with the encouragement or coercion of the colonial government. There were clear differences in the structures of government introduced by the different colonial powers, with the civil-law countries favouring a more assimilationist approach, and the British preferring where they could to co-opt pre-existing institutions to the system that became known as indirect rule. But there were also commonalities. Institutions were created that for the most part followed the logic of what Europeans called 'tribe', grouping together people whom the colonizers (and their anthropologists) decided had a common language and culture. 'Chiefs' of these groups, approved or created by the colonizers, were authorized to take lower-level decisions affecting their own ethnic subjects. The higher-level courts and administrators backed up this authority (so long as there was no challenge to the colonizers' power), based where necessary on their own interpretation of the relevant 'customary' law. Individuals who found themselves outside the geographical zone of the 'tribe' to which it was determined they belonged could be doubly disadvantaged. These migrants benefited neither from the legal rights given those subject to 'European' law, nor from the 'customary' protections given those who could make a claim on a particular 'tribal' leader.[3]

At independence, the laws of the new states were designed to reassert the equal rights of all races and ethnicities. New citizenship laws were adopted, largely based on models from the power that had colonized them, but using the versions that had applied at home to their own full citizens rather than in their colonies. As in other regions of the world, these new laws generally based the right to citizenship on a combination of descent from parents who themselves were citizens and the fact of birth in the country. Though gender bias was a common feature of these laws – as it was at the time in the European states – formal equality between races was the norm. The term 'native' itself was reappropriated in the former British colonies to be a term of pride and not denigration (though the same did not happen to *indigène* in French).

To a great extent this process was both necessary and positive. The reclaiming of political and economic space sometimes went further, however: beyond steps to create equality before the law and to redress the economic and political inequalities that the colonial era had created, to measures that excluded those who had arrived in the wake of empire from the right to protection by the new state at all. Some of the countries most affected by migration created rules for membership that explicitly or implicitly denied citizenship to people whose parents had been immigrants – but who themselves had been born in the country and knew no other home. As 'native' became a positive label, 'settler' came to be a term of abuse.

Transitional rules were of course needed everywhere to cater for the handover of legal authority from the colonial power to the new states. Although international law is clear on the basic principle that individuals who were ordinarily resident in the former state become nationals of the new state, the rules were in some cases written or rewritten to exclude those who were asserted to have insufficient 'historical' connection to the territory concerned. Many of the problems related to citizenship rights described in this book have their root causes in the manipulation and exploitation of the rules that governed the transition to independence. A number of states from the outset aimed to exclude from citizenship those who could not claim an ancestral link to the land; and several others amended their laws in the years after independence to strengthen a racial or ethnic element in the law. The detail of the dates at which a person's ancestor arrived in the country became of critical importance to their rights today.

Thus, citizenship laws were written in many new African states that introduced rules specifically designed to exclude recent migrants from full citizenship rights; and in particular to exclude the descendants of European and Asian immigrants from citizenship by birth, even if they might have the right to naturalize. In some countries (Uganda and the Democratic Republic of Congo) the constitution itself still limits those who may be citizens by birth to the ethnic groups present in the country on a particular date, with many arguments about what that date should be; in others (Sierra Leone and Liberia) only those 'of negro descent' can be full citizens; in yet others (among them Nigeria) there is an implied preference for the native over the immigrant in citizenship laws that require descent from ancestors who were born in the country.

A similar distrust was applied to those potential citizens of the new states who might have a claim on another passport; the great majority of African countries prohibited dual citizenship either at or soon after independence (though the rules have often changed in recent years). They wished to ensure that those who might have a claim on another citizenship – especially those of European, Asian or Middle Eastern descent – had to choose between their two possible loyalties. Those who did not take the citizenship of the newly independent country were then regarded with suspicion, as a possible 'fifth column' for the former colonial powers and other interests.

Not coincidentally, these rules were most problematic in those countries where colonial-era migration and dispossession of land had been most marked, where the numbers of those who had arrived during empire remaining after independence were largest, and where the political power of those affected was weakest. As happened later following the collapse of the Soviet Union, when the European empires in Africa retreated they left behind a legacy of resentment of incomers and their privileges that still reverberates today. But the migration of the first half of the twentieth century was not only of Europeans and Asians: hundreds of thousands of Africans also moved, sometimes under duress, as a result of the political and economic changes brought by colonization. Despite the strong rhetoric of African solidarity that all governments express, these migrants also find their right to citizenship and belonging under threat today.

Some of the most egregious cases of citizenship discrimination in Africa are described in detail in this book. They illustrate the consequences for peace and security of national citizenship law, policy and rhetoric that found their structure on an ethnic or racial basis; the use and abuse of citizenship law to silence political opponents; and the everyday injustice to ordinary people that results. Though it is tempting for politicians all over the world to mobilize an 'in-group' of supporters by blaming an 'out-group' of alleged foreigners for all their troubles, the consequences of a focus on blood-and-soil connection to the country can be disastrous not only for that group, but for the country as a whole.

Denationalized groups

In the Democratic Republic of Congo (DRC), the disputed 'indigenous' or 'non-indigenous' status of the Banyarwanda populations (speaking dialects of the Kinyarwanda language centred on modern-day Rwanda) of the eastern provinces has been at the heart of the conflicts that have afflicted the region. Disputes over the law have been at the heart of the wider debate. The changing balance of political power at national level has been reflected first in the decision to create an ethnic definition for citizenship in the constitution, and then in the repeatedly amended laws that have shifted the 'date of origin' for an ethnic group to qualify for citizenship back and forth with the political tide. At different times, this date was set at 1885 (the date of creation of the Belgian king's personal colony, the 'Congo Free State'), 1908 (the date the colony was transferred to the Belgian state), 1950 and 1960 (the date of independence). Those excluded by these laws form the core of the rebel groups that have challenged central authority since the late 1990s.

This ethnic focus has its roots in population displacements of the years under colonial rule. Although parts of the territory that is now DRC (formerly Zaire) were, prior to colonization, already occupied by Kinyarwanda speakers, the Belgian colonial authorities greatly increased these numbers by transplanting tens of thousands of people from the already densely populated

Rwanda and Burundi to eastern Congo to form a source of labour for commercial agricultural plantations. Then, at the moment of independence, eastern Congo also took in huge numbers of refugees fleeing violence in Rwanda and Burundi (sadly, a pattern to be repeated).

The status of the Banyarwanda was thus already of key importance in the jockeying for position among different ethnic groups during the lead-up to independence. In 1964, the first constitution adopted by the new state declared that to qualify as a Congolese citizen a person had to have an ancestor who was 'a member of a tribe or part of a tribe established in the Congo before 18 October 1908' – thus excluding those who had come under the Belgian population transfers. During the 1970s, the law was changed to provide more recent dates; but in 1981 a new code of nationality included only those who could show that their ancestors were established in the country when its borders were first set in 1885. With the arrival of hundreds of thousands of refugees in the aftermath of the Rwandan genocide, resentment of this influx and of the Rwandan army interventions that followed built to the point where the national parliament adopted a resolution declaring all Banyarwanda to be foreigners who had acquired citizenship fraudulently. Two successive rebellions plunged the country into a decade of war, in which half a dozen of Congo's neighbours also became involved.

The terms agreed in a peace deal in 2004 form the basis of the new constitution and citizenship law, which recognize as a Congolese citizen by birth 'every person belonging to the ethnic groups and nationalities of which the individuals and territory formed what became Congo at independence'. Yet active hostilities still continue in the east, and the status of the different Banyarwanda as indigenes or non-indigenes remains central to that conflict. Despite the date change to 1960, the law still founds the basis of Congolese nationality on ethnicity, rather than on birth, residence or other objective criteria; meaning that the argument still centres on claims to ancestral origin and bloodline. Hate speech and exclusion flourish in this legal environment.

9

In Côte d'Ivoire, meanwhile, the instability and civil war that have devastated the country's once prosperous economy since 1999, displacing some 750,000 people and causing 3 million to require humanitarian assistance, have some of their deepest roots in conflicts over the definition of who is a 'real' citizen of the country. Central to the peace negotiations has been a regularization of nationality status.

During the 1930s, the French colonial authorities both modified borders and encouraged the movement of several hundred thousand agricultural workers from what are now Burkina Faso and Mali south to fertile land in what was to become Côte d'Ivoire. While Côte d'Ivoire enjoyed a post-independence economic boom, the status of this group was relatively uncontroversial; but from the mid-1990s, as economic conditions deteriorated with a decline in global commodity prices, the status of the 'non-indigenous' population – estimated in the 1998 census to form 26 per cent of the total – became increasingly contested. Once northerner Alassane Ouattara tried to run for president, southern politicians increasingly mobilized rhetoric and law to insinuate that anyone with a possible northern support base was in essence a foreigner. Ouattara himself was said to have a parent from Burkina Faso, and the law was changed to require both parents of a presidential candidate to be Ivorian by origin. Meanwhile, those ordinary people alleged to be migrants faced ever-increasing difficulties in obtaining the necessary identity cards and certificates of nationality to claim their other citizenship rights, including voting, registration of children in school, running businesses and owning land.

A Christmas Eve military coup in 1999 was followed by deeply flawed elections in late 2000. Southern leaders deployed both administrative measures and violence to exclude from voting or standing for office those of migrant origin as well as northerners and Muslims deemed suspect by association. This exclusion brought a rebellion, a period of active civil war and the de facto partition of the country into two zones, a partition that continues today.

Guillaume Soro, leader of the rebel New Forces, emphasized the foundation of the war in citizenship rights by stating: 'Give us our identity cards and we hand over our Kalashnikovs.' Citizenship issues have been among the core questions to be resolved in the negotiations to end the war. A programme of identification through public hearings before magistrates had by May 2008 issued new documents to 600,000 of some 3.5 million Ivorians believed to be eligible. Yet these documents were only the basis for a nationality application, and not confirmation of nationality itself. Continuing problems with the identification system meant that elections were in late 2008 postponed once again to the next year as the voters' register could not be completed.

In Zimbabwe, the different structure of the colonial state has brought a different type of conflict over the issue of 'who belongs'. Though what was formerly Rhodesia ceased to be a British colony in 1961, majority rule was obtained only in 1980, following a bitter guerrilla war in which the right to land was as much an issue as the right to vote. Ultimately, the war was ended by negotiation, and an official policy of reconciliation left the wealthy white population largely undisturbed. Land reform was undertaken, but thanks to the terms of the peace settlement was required to be on a 'willing-seller, willing-buyer' basis for the first decade. Nevertheless, measures were progressively taken to require white Zimbabweans to declare their loyalty to the new state, principally by focusing on and denying their possible right to other citizenships.

Although the 1980 Zimbabwean constitution allowed dual citizenship, the 1984 Citizenship of Zimbabwe Act introduced a prohibition on dual citizenship, together with a requirement that Zimbabwean citizens with an entitlement to another citizenship renounce that right. An estimated 30,000 whites renounced their foreign citizenship before Zimbabwean officials and kept or obtained Zimbabwean passports as a result.

As the popularity of the government of President Robert Mugabe declined, the ban on dual citizenship was taken to absurd extremes as part of an effort to blame others for the country's economic decline. The unexpected success of the opposition in a February 2000 constitutional referendum and June 2000 parliamentary elections led the ruling party to seek to disenfranchise the groups it most blamed for the results: white Zimbabweans, as well as around 200,000 farm workers working on white-owned farms. In 2001, the government amended the citizenship law to require those with a possible claim to another citizenship to renounce it under the relevant foreign law as well as under Zimbabwean law – even if they had never in fact held a passport or identity document from any other country but Zimbabwe. Surreal interactions ensued at the embassies of Malawi, Mozambique, Britain and other countries, where those whom the Zimbabwean government alleged had an entitlement to foreign citizenship tried to find a way to renounce a non-existent status. And in subsequent elections these alleged non-citizens found themselves unable to vote.

In Sierra Leone, as in its neighbour Liberia, an economically advantaged group have found themselves excluded in a less dramatic but similar way. The 1961 independence constitution of Sierra Leone followed the standard model for British colonies and created a single nationality without any distinction by race, ethnic group or sex. Within a year after independence, the constitutional provisions on citizenship were amended to insert a requirement that only a person 'of negro African descent' – defined as having a father or grandfather 'of negro African descent', thus adding gender to race discrimination – could be a citizen of the new country. Subsequent laws restricted the rights of non-citizens to acquire property or carry out certain businesses.

The change to the law was directed against the less than 1 per cent of the country's population known collectively as 'Lebanese', whose parents and grandparents settled in Sierra Leone from the Middle East. In particular, the motivation was to exclude Lebanese and mixed-race Sierra Leoneans from the right to contest for office in the 1962 elections. Although John Akar, a prominent Sierra Leonean whose mother was a black Sierra Leonean and father of Lebanese origin, argued in court all the way to the Privy Council in London that the amendments were unconstitutional, and won the case, the government simply re enacted the law and abolished the right to appeal from the Sierra Leonean courts. The distinctions were retained in the 1973 citizenship law that is still in force today. Those with Lebanese fathers were excluded from citizenship in the land of their birth and the only home they had ever had. Only in 2006 was the law reformed to end gender discrimination; but the requirement that at least one parent or grandparent had to be of 'negro African descent' was retained.

At its most extreme, governments have simply expelled en masse those alleged to be non-citizens. The best-known case of mass expulsion in Africa is that of the Ugandan Asians driven out of the country by the government of Idi Amin. Yet many other African countries have also expelled citizens en masse, often in appalling conditions, and without any right to a hearing. Uganda itself, in a much less well-known episode that took place under President Milton Obote, displaced a large number of Banyarwanda (many of them tracing their ancestry to the Ugandan side of the border) in the early 1980s. Among the most egregious cases described in this book are the expulsion of tens of thousands of Ethiopians of Eritrean descent who had their Ethiopian nationality arbitrarily cancelled and nationality documents destroyed, before their forced expulsion to Eritrea following the eruption of war between the two states in 1998 – and tens of thousands of Eritreans of Ethiopian descent subject to reciprocal expulsions in the other direction; and the expulsion of around 75,000 black Mauritanians from their country in 1989 and 1990. Numerous other countries have periodically engaged in sweeps to expel first-generation migrants.

Less dramatic but more widespread is denial of citizenship rights by bureaucracy. The discretion given to administrative officials in the individual small decisions to issue identity documents or passports, accept an application for naturalization, or add someone to the electoral or the school roll means that those perceived as outsiders can be effectively excluded from the benefits of citizenship even if their nationality is never formally taken away. Members of these groups across Africa report difficulties in getting travel documents, voting, holding on to their land, or accessing public services supposedly available to all. Frequently these problems are exacerbated by a gender discrimination that means that the children of a woman who 'married out' are regarded as not being full members of the community. An absence of necessary documentation to prove citizenship then has the same effect as a formally adopted law denying citizenship; with the added disadvantage that each person affected has to fight separately for her rights, rather than being able to mobilize collectively in one single battle on the principles at stake.

The same problems of citizenship at national level are often repeated within African states at provincial or local level. An individual from (or descended from parents who are from) another part of the country, or from an ethnic group that crosses the border between two provinces, will not be regarded as being eligible for full rights within that province. Just as at the national level, disputes over who 'owns' a province can lead to violence and breakdown of civil order. In some cases, well-intentioned efforts to address the challenges of multiethnicity have made the situation worse.

In Nigeria, for example, the federal constitution has over the years been altered to create more and more federating states, now numbering thirty-six, effectively though not explicitly on the basis of ethnicity (though sometimes several ethnic groups have to share one state). There are also provisions requiring that each government structure reflect the 'federal character' of Nigeria, and include officials who are representative of all the groups that are 'indigenous' to the federation or to the state or local government area. But these measures intended to promote inclusivity have created a position where, within each state, those who are not members of an ethnic group 'from' the state – who have moved from another part of Nigeria or who are the children of those who have migrated – are not regarded as being 'indigenous' to the state, and not entitled to the state benefits resulting from the 'federal character' provisions. They cannot stand for office, are not eligible for state education scholarships or other grants, and increasingly may not obtain jobs in the civil service of the state. This system has inadvertently created a population of millions who are not regarded as full citizens in any particular place in Nigeria. Though they may vote, there is no state in which they may hold public office and take part in the government of their country. Perhaps the only public office open to them would be the presidency itself; though in practice that, too, would be difficult without a clear support base in an individual state.

Ethiopia, the only other fully federal constitution in Africa, remarkably provides for any self-defined group to make a bid for self-determination, up to and including complete independence. But the results of this effort to give full realization to minority rights have included the displacement of large numbers of people from areas now 'owned' by another group, where they then feel threatened. There are similar problems in many countries without explicitly federal constitutions, especially those that are most diverse; notably, the DRC. The ethnic violence following the disputed Kenyan elections of late 2007 had among its causes a persistent failure by government to provide an equitable process to resolve the rights to land and to protection of the law of those living in a different part of the country from their 'original' home.

Silencing individuals

Citizenship law has also proved a useful tool to incumbent governments wishing to silence critics, or exclude from elections opposition politicians who threaten to unseat them. A wide range of African governments have used, abused or rewritten citizenship and immigration law to silence those who have criticized them or sought to challenge their hold on power. They have changed the qualifications for citizenship, or simply asserted that someone is not a citizen and then deported them, with no right to challenge in court either the deportation or the assertion of non-citizenship. Although there are other means of silencing journalists and blocking political candidates, denationalization has the particular usefulness of effectively taking the individual outside the realm of legal rights and into what is claimed to be an area of exclusive and discretionary executive power.

In Côte d'Ivoire, Alassane Ouattara was just the most famous victim of a general citizenship crisis. But these cases are not confined to those countries that have become notorious for citizenship conflict. In Botswana, one of Africa's longest-standing democracies, John Modise found his right to citizenship by descent denied once he founded an opposition political party. Although the government allowed him citizenship by naturalization, the presidency in Botswana is restricted to citizens by birth or descent. Born in South Africa of Batswana parents prior to the independence of Botswana, he had been brought up in Botswana. Expelled from Botswana in 1978 and declared an 'undesirable immigrant' once his political ambitions were apparent, he was deported and redeported to and from South Africa and its nominally 'independent' homeland of Bophuthatswana, spending years in a Kafkaesque legal limbo that effectively quashed his political aspirations. A complaint lodged with the African Commission on Human and Peoples' Rights in 1993 was eventually decided in his favour in 2000; but too late to have any practical effect on his ability to run for public office.

In Zambia, a new constitution adopted in 1996 by the Movement for Multiparty Democracy (MMD) government elected in 1991 introduced a requirement that both parents of any presidential candidate must be Zambians by birth. The intention, as everyone understood, was to disqualify former president Kenneth Kaunda from standing for the presidency in the 1996 elections on the ticket of the United National Independence Party (UNIP), since his parents had been missionaries from what later became Malawi. Even without this amendment, in 1994 the MMD government had abused citizenship and immigration laws to deport two other leading UNIP politicians, William Steven Banda and John Lyson Chinula, on the grounds that they were not citizens and were 'likely to be a danger to peace and good order'. The African

Commission on Human and Peoples' Rights ruled against the Zambian government in both Kaunda's and Banda and Chinula's cases – but again not in time to enable them to contest for political office when they wished.

The Tanzanian government, despite its mostly positive record, has also attempted to use citizenship law to denationalize several journalists and other critics. In 2001, the government declared four individuals – including Jenerali Ulimwengu, a leading publisher, journalist and media proprietor; and the country's then high commissioner to Nigeria, Timothy Bandora – to be noncitizens. In 2006, the government again stripped two journalists of their nationality, accusing them of being 'unpatriotic and enemies of the state'.

These cases continue. In Zimbabwe, as in Côte d'Ivoire, a general programme of denationalization has had the benefit of providing scope for the government also to silence troublesome individuals (or simply to humiliate past enemies). In December 2005, the Zimbabwean government informed Trevor Ncube, owner of two independent newspapers that were highly critical of President Mugabe's policies, that he had forfeited his Zimbabwean citizenship because he had failed to renounce his Zambian citizenship – which he had never claimed but was allegedly entitled to because his father was born in Zambia. Ncube's passport was restored to him following a court order. Others who had their passports taken away for good included the last Rhodesian prime minister, Ian Smith, and his predecessor Sir Garfield Todd, deposed as head of government when he tried to liberalize Rhodesia's apartheid-style rule – and then also deprived of his passport by Ian Smith's government. Judith Todd, daughter of Garfield Todd and herself a high-profile opponent of the former white minority regime and an activist under the new government, was also deprived of her passport on the basis that she had a notional entitlement to New Zealand citizenship.

The scale of the problem

The true number of people affected by the crisis of citizenship and statelessness in Africa is difficult to estimate, but they are certainly in the millions and possibly in the tens of millions. The largest groups include at least a quarter of Côte d'Ivoire's 17 million people; several hundred thousand Banyarwanda in the DRC; hundreds of thousands of Zimbabweans of European or Malawian, Mozambican and other African descent; around 150,000 Ethiopians of Eritrean descent still living in Ethiopia; around 25,000 black Mauritanians expelled from their country in 1989/90 who were as of early 2007 still refugees (though a repatriation process began under a new Mauritanian government in 2007, the process was thrown into doubt by an August 2008 military coup); perhaps 50,000 Muslims in Madagascar; thousands of Sierra Leoneans of Lebanese descent; and tens of thousands of Ugandans of Asian descent. Moreover, there are uncountable numbers of people with a citizen mother and foreign father who are denied citizenship in all those countries in Africa that still discriminate on the basis of gender in the right to pass citizenship to children (at least sixteen states on paper; many more in administrative practice).

Added to these totals must be long-term refugees in countries that do not recognize the right of refugees to naturalize after a period of residence: these include tens of thousands of refugees in Egypt, especially those of Palestinian origin, as well as the more than a hundred thousand refugees from the Moroccan-occupied territory of Western Sahara, largely still living in camps in Algeria, with identity documents issued by a liberation movement which are recognized only by a small minority of countries, most of them African.

Moreover, many would include in the list of those who are effectively stateless those Africans who are members of pastoralist, hunter-gatherer or other nomad populations who find themselves on the margins of African states, often the object of government suspicion or excluded from the benefits of citizenship. Their legal status as citizens may not be officially denied, but they operate essentially beyond the reach of state structures and the rights to political participation and legal and social protection that citizenship should provide.

Some countries have populations in all categories: in Kenya, for example, Asian Kenyans came with colonization and had their citizenship rights restricted at various times; Nubian Kenyans are black Africans yet still regarded as not eligible for full Kenyan citizenship because they 'originally' came from somewhere else; the ethnic Somali population has been consistently suspected of support for pan-Somali unity and subject to security-force harassment and denial of citizenship rights as a result; nomadic pastoralist populations are excluded from many of the public services that are extended to other Kenyans. Refugees hosted in Kenya are in practice largely excluded from naturalizing as citizens, while children born outside the country with just a Kenyan mother cannot claim citizenship, though children with a Kenyan father can do so.

Among these groups, some individuals have had recognition of their citizenship in the form of documents that were later invalidated by the state; some still hold citizenship documents but are in danger of losing them at any time; some have never had citizenship documents but would encounter difficulties or denial if they tried to obtain them; and some hold documents, but suffer legally mandated restrictions or discrimination that denies them equal treatment with other citizens. All of them are vulnerable because the legal basis of their rights – citizenship – is non-existent, in question or under threat.

The flawed argument from 'I was here first'

The principal argument used to deny full citizenship to the (relatively) recent migrants to and within Africa is that they are not really 'from' the place. The independent states of Africa need the undivided loyalty of their citizens, and the loyalties of these 'immigrant' groups or those of mixed parentage are suspect because of their presumed divided identities.

Yet the same states that deny the right of those descended

from the migrants of the nineteenth and twentieth centuries to be citizens of the new states have argued against the rights to any special recognition for those Africans who claim the same title of 'indigenous people' as Aboriginal Australians, Native Americans and others. Often nomadic and hunter-gatherer in terms of their economic base, these populations were displaced first by the settled African populations that arrived many centuries later, and then again by European colonization during the eighteenth and nineteenth centuries.

Although in Australasia and the Americas increasing mobilization has brought greater recognition of the rights of 'indigenous peoples' within the context of the international human rights movement, in Africa the concept of 'indigenous peoples' used in this way is highly contested.

The Botswana government, for example, denies that the Basarwa or Bushmen, descendants of peoples who migrated to southern Africa many thousands of years before the ancestors of today's dominant ethnic groups followed, should have any special recognition as a result. In particular, the government resists any suggestion that these 'older' natives may have rights that are not fulfilled by the democratic election to power of the 'newer' natives in place of the 'newest' (white) settlers and by the imposition of that group's conception of appropriate lifestyles for Botswanan citizens. Yet, turned on its head in a different historical outcome, the Basarwa could make the same arguments against the 'settler' Tswana as the government of Zimbabwe today uses against its white citizens.

The sensitivity over prior claims to being 'indigenous' that may be argued to give them rights over those regarded as 'natives' by the European colonizers is shared by sufficient African states for the African Union to be extremely nervous about efforts by the United Nations (UN) to adopt a Declaration on the Rights of Indigenous Peoples. African heads of state adopted a resolution in January 2007 in response to this initiative, affirming that 'the vast majority of the peoples of Africa are indigenous to the African continent'.

The complications of this argument illustrate the difficulty of basing citizenship rights on the playground principle of 'I was here first'. The reality is that in today's globalized world millions of people can trace ancestry to two or more different locations. Sometimes those locations are thousands of kilometres apart across the ocean; sometimes just the other side of a political border created for the first time a century or a decade ago. Many people of African descent are fighting for their rights to be fully acknowledged as citizens in the countries that previously colonized Africa.

Beyond citizenship law

The stories told in this book are partial histories, of course: the issues at stake in the civil wars in Congo and Côte d'Ivoire, in the old-fashioned interstate clash between Eritrea and Ethiopia, or in the discrimination against Europeans, Lebanese or Asians in Zimbabwe, Sierra Leone and Uganda are not restricted to the legal definition of who is a citizen of the states concerned. Citizenship law has been used as a tool to get at issues of economic and political power: control of land, commercial opportunities and public office. Extreme violence and discrimination are possible without any abuse of citizenship law to support their deployment, as the 1994 genocide in Rwanda shows. Marginalized groups can be excluded from *effective* exercise of citizenship rights even if their right to *legal* citizenship in itself is not contested, notably in the case of individuals subjected to slavery or its contemporary variations, or ethnic groups following a different lifestyle from the national norm, including nomads such as pastoralists or hunter-gatherers. The application of citizenship law may reflect as much as reinforce these and other deep-seated cultural beliefs or prejudices that exclude individuals from full participation in a community; perhaps most obviously in the case of gender discrimination.

There is a vast literature on the nature of nationalism and nation-building, identity, race, ethnicity, gender, autochthony and the politics of belonging, both in Africa and worldwide,

21

which attempts to grapple with these broader questions. Feminist writings in particular have pointed out that the concept of citizenship should move beyond the lawyer's link between individual and state to encompass ideas of individual autonomy and freedom to engage on a basis of equality in all aspects of public and private life. Notions of belonging and the right (or lack of it) to make claims on any particular community go far beyond the strictly legal or official, and operate at local and regional as well as national levels, and in terms of larger units as well. Individuals can have claims akin to what lawyers call citizenship on other entities, whether town or region or, in Africa in particular, on the structures of governance that operate at the level of ethnic group. Individuals and communities at the margins of African states may find these structures far more important – for good or ill – than the state itself. In African countries where the state is weakest, or most predatory, the idea of national citizenship may be irrelevant to most people most of the time.

Yet this book argues that a denial of the right to citizenship itself under national law is often central to the denial of other rights; and not only because of the symbolic value of the law in establishing public discourse. Ethnic and gender discrimination in citizenship law may exclude those affected not only from the right to vote and hold public office, but also from the right to access education, health and other goods, as well as from the right to freedom of movement. They have effects far beyond the question of individual legal status.

These effects are felt even in those states that have abandoned their supposed role of physical and social protection and even when the supposedly more powerful are targeted. The allegations in North Kivu that the Banyarwanda are not 'really' Congolese, the insistence of President Mugabe that white Zimbabweans are 'really' tools for the recolonization of the country by the British, or the denial of citizenship to 'Lebanese' Sierra Leoneans have their power because they are based in resentment of past and present control over land and other economic resources. But the impact of the citizenship law discrimination is just as real and just as unjust for the individuals affected, whatever the history may be. And the denial of citizenship to these groups means that in practice the issues of land and economic inequality are actually (perhaps even deliberately) made more difficult to resolve. Not only are the minds of those who should be governing the country or resolving the conflict distracted from serious attempts to address the underlying problems, but the validity of the participation of those who must be a part of the solution is denied. And without their participation, the other problems can only remain intractable, harming all who live in the state.

Redefining national citizenship

Different approaches to citizenship are possible, even in countries that are just as multiethnic as Côte d'Ivoire, DRC or Kenya. Citizenship is a dynamic concept, the notion of 'who belongs' surprisingly flexible over time, especially where those in authority lead the effort to redefine the rules. And those African countries that have taken an inclusive approach to citizenship, providing for a wide access to those who are born in their country, have been among the most peaceful since independence. Tanzania, one of the few African countries that provides citizenship to anyone born on its territory, has over the years repeatedly taken steps to integrate migrant and refugee populations to full citizenship rights, and has benefited with social peace. Several of the francophone countries of the West African Sahel provide non-discriminatory and generous provisions for citizenship for those born in the country, even though birth in the country does not provide citizenship in itself.

A trickle of reforms since the mid-1990s has brought increasing gender equality to citizenship law, even though a majority of African countries still do not allow women to pass citizenship to both their husbands and children on an equal basis with men. The steady changes to the rules on dual citizenship also provide cause for hope. Increasingly, African countries have relaxed their prohibitions on dual citizenship to allow their own diasporas now in Europe or North America to retain their links to the country

23

of nationality of their parents or grandparents. Roughly half of African states now allow dual nationality. The lobbying of these individuals with economic power has brought a political maturity to their states of ethnic origin in matters of citizenship where years of protest by European or South Asian governments at discriminatory treatment of their own emigrants to Africa had only a counterproductive effect. Though dual nationality will only ever be exercised by a minority in any state, those who hold two passports can provide a concrete demonstration that it is not necessary to have a 'pure' bloodline to be a good citizen.

South Africa, home of the most extreme version of the settler–native divide embodied in the notion of apartheid, had farthest to go to dismantle this system of discrimination and has achieved the greatest transformation of its legal system. In place of a baroque multiplication of different classes of citizenship based on race and ethnicity – both given an entirely inappropriate 'scientific' basis – the 1996 constitution creates a single united citizenship, and the rights of all citizens are equal. The new government sought to address the economic and political legacy of the past by offering citizenship to many long-term migrants brought to South Africa under apartheid labour policies; and by measures of affirmative action and economic empowerment for black people, rather than by denying the rights of those who had previously held power to be citizens at all. A new refugee law provided for the right to asylum and eventual grant of citizenship to recognized refugees. The Constitutional Court has confirmed that even non-citizens have certain claims upon the state for social protection.

South Africa also provides perhaps the most vivid illustration of the truth that adopting new laws is only a first step towards overcoming past and present injustice. The promise of the new democracy has been sorely tested by the continuing challenge of domestic racial inequality and racial prejudice, as well as by massive popular resentment at large-scale migration from elsewhere in Africa. In May and June 2008, ordinary South Africans erupted in violence that targeted African refugees and migrants: more than sixty people died, and thousands were displaced. The official response was inadequate and sometimes abusive in practice. Then-president Thabo Mbeki, who had famously stated and re-stated his identification as 'an African' at the time of the adoption of the post-apartheid constitution, was inexplicably slow to speak out against the violence. Yet the leaders of the ruling African National Congress and most other senior politicians have largely continued to condemn xenophobia and re-emphasize the values of that constitution. Keeping to the vision of the 1955 Freedom Charter that 'South Africa belongs to all who live in it, black and white' will no doubt remain a challenge; abandoning it is a sure route to chaos. And integration of the Freedom Charter's vision into the laws of other countries could provide the basis for resolution of some of the most bitter conflicts Africa has faced.

The Freedom Charter

We, the People of South Africa, declare for all our country and the world to know:

That South Africa belongs to all who live in it, black and white, and that no government can justly claim authority unless it is based on the will of all the people ...

Adopted at the Congress of the People, Kliptown, South Africa, 26 June 1955

---

2 | Empire to independence: the evolution of citizenship law in Africa

The norms that governed membership of the previous African polities were largely wiped out by the sudden expansion in the late nineteenth century of the European powers' coastal trading enclaves to become full-blown imperial territories. Though these systems survived and continued to have immense influence on the daily lives of Africans, for the colonizers their legal effect was for the most part at sub-national scale only. The colonial powers might pay attention to an interpretation of 'customary' rules when their courts came to be used to settle disputes among their African subjects, but they had little relevance to the determination of an individual's membership of the colonial state, which was determined by the European power with control of the territory.

During the age of empire the grant of nationality was (as it is still for the most part) regarded under international law as being within the discretion of the state concerned; though it was generally assumed that if you were born in a territory you had the nationality of that state. At the same time, nationality in itself did not necessarily give the individual concerned full rights within the state, since it was accepted that only a limited few could participate fully in its government. Women in particular were in most places excluded from full citizenship rights in the countries of which they were nationals until at least the early twentieth century. In the colonial states of Africa and elsewhere, all those not of European descent were similarly disadvantaged. Citizenship law and practice ensured that all but a tiny number of Africans were subordinate in status to the white-skinned citizens of the colonial states.[1]

A rhetoric of service, of carrying the 'white man's burden', of bringing civilization and Christianity to the 'dark continent', thus could not disguise – at least not to those at the sharp end of the process – the essential exploitation of colonial rule and the crudeness of the efforts to make the African colonies pay for themselves with their resources. To be a 'native' (*indigène*) was to be an inferior being whose culture was denigrated, who had no right to influence the decision-making processes that governed daily life, whose property was regularly forfeited, and who had only limited civil liberties protections. Only a tiny minority of Africans ever achieved the right to be treated on the same legal basis as whites; a status known in the French colonies as *évolué* or in the Portuguese as *assimilado*.

Africans born in most of the British territories in Africa were officially known as 'British protected persons', a status that provided some rights but was a lesser status than that of 'British subject', applied to those born in the British Isles and their descendants. A British protected person was governed by what was applied as customary law, rules largely not written down but interpreted by the colonial courts on the basis of 'native' interlocutors with an override for those customs believed to contravene British conceptions of 'moral repugnancy'. A British subject – known as a 'citizen of the United Kingdom and colonies' after the first great reform of British nationality law in 1948 – was governed by the common law and statute, with the same civil and political rights as those born and living in Great Britain.

In the colonies of the civil-law countries the same basic division existed, though differently encoded. In the French colonies of north and sub-Saharan Africa, those with full French citizenship (*citoyens français à part entière*) were those who had moved to Africa from France itself and their descendants, including those of mixed race, plus a small number of Africans resident in particular privileged towns. The vast majority of residents of French colonial territories were French subjects (*sujets français*). French subjects were governed by the *code de l'indigénat*, a set of laws first established in Algeria in 1887 and in force until about the end of the Second World War, which established the inferior legal status of *indigènes* and provided for the application of local customary law to them, as interpreted by colonial courts. The five Portuguese colonies similarly had two categories of citizenship, encoded from 1899: the *indígena* (native) and the *não-indígena* (non-native). The *não-indígenas*, European-born Portuguese and white-skinned foreigners, were full Portuguese citizens subjected to metropolitan laws, whereas the *indígenas* were administered by the 'customary' laws of each territory. Belgium and Spain had similar rules. Only in the very last days of empire did France and Portugal offer full citizenship to a much larger number of colonial subjects, at their option.

Conditions varied among the various territories, but in all the natives or 'indigenes' were obliged to pay specific taxes in kind or in cash, often forced to work, and required to obtain a pass to leave the country or to travel internally. The non-natives, meanwhile, could leave the country freely, were exempt from labour legislation and paid taxes in their home countries. In addition, different residents of the colonial territories were subject to very different rights in relation to land ownership. For example, Africans in the British colonies deemed suitable for European settlement – South Africa, Rhodesia and Kenya in particular – were confined to 'native reserves' where they could hold land under customary law; whereas only Europeans could have freehold title in the fertile lands designated for their settlement. Africans were brought in as labourers but denied the right to own land themselves. The apogee of such distinctions was reached in South Africa, where the self-governing and subsequently fully independent country built from the mid-twentieth century a legal framework of extraordinarily complex race- and ethnicity-based citizenship distinctions. A majority of black South Africans had even their nominal nationality taken away, told that instead they belonged to one of ten supposedly independent ethnically designated 'homelands'.

This history meant that at independence there was particular resentment of the population groups that had arrived as a result of imperial conquest: not only of the whites themselves, but also of groups that had arrived in their wake, including even those whose origins were in other parts of Africa. Thus, the rules governing the transition to independence were particularly sensitive in the context of citizenship law. Many of the cases described in this book deal with the status of those who were recognized as colonial subjects but whose presence is challenged today; or with the determination of where someone belongs whose parents came from different parts of a common colonial territory.

The basic rule in international law relating to citizenship in the context of such 'state successions' is that those who were living in the territory concerned automatically acquire the nationality of the new state and lose their former nationality; though the new state still has the right to decide in detail whom it will regard as its nationals. International law does not compel states to *grant* their nationality except in very limited cases (for example, to children who would otherwise be stateless). The international human rights treaties adopted since the establishment of the United Nations (many of them during the same period in which African countries were gaining independence) do, however, limit the previously assumed absolute state discretion over citizenship, by requiring states to work to reduce statelessness, and by prohibiting discrimination in granting citizenship and arbitrary deprivation of citizenship.

Accordingly, at independence citizenship of most of the new states was in principle granted on an equal footing to individuals of different racial and ethnic groups. The new states' citizenship laws were to a large extent based on models from the power that had colonized them; of course, using the versions that had applied to their own full citizens rather than to the 'natives' in their colonies.[2]

In the former colonies of Britain, where nationality law had not been codified at all until 1948, the constitutions of the new states of what was now called the Commonwealth were drafted according to a standard template, known as the 'Lancaster House' model after the building in London where they were negotiated. According to these constitutions people born in the former protectorate who had been citizens of the United Kingdom and colonies or British protected persons automatically became citizens of the new state, unless neither of their parents nor any of their grandparents were born there. Those born in the country whose parents and grandparents were born outside became entitled to the status of citizen by birth and could register to be accorded it as of right; while others who were potential citizens could apply to naturalize.

In both francophone and lusophone countries the civil code was adopted, based on their respective models. From 1889, the French Civil Code provided that a child born in France of one parent also born in France became French; while a child born in France of foreign parents could claim citizenship at majority. Just as the anglophone countries' citizenship laws followed a common pattern, the *codes de la nationalité* adopted by the francophone countries of west Africa mostly still resemble this model both in their content and in the format they follow. In the lusophone countries also, which obtained independence only in 1975 with the end of dictatorship in Portugal, content and form tend towards a similar pattern.

Both the common-law and the civil-law models of citizenship that came to be applied in Africa generally combine the two basic concepts known as *jus soli* (literally, law or right of the soil), whereby an individual obtains citizenship because he or she was born in a particular country, and *jus sanguinis* (law/right of blood), where citizenship is based on descent from parents who themselves are citizens. In general, a law based on *jus sanguinis* will tend to exclude from citizenship those who are descended from individuals who have migrated from one place to another. An exclusive *jus soli* rule, on the other hand, would prevent individuals from claiming the citizenship of their parents if they had moved away from their 'historical' home, but is more inclusive of the actual residents of a particular territory.

A handful of African countries today give automatic citizenship on a *jus soli* basis to any child born on their soil, though more than twenty give citizenship to children born in their territory of non-citizen parents who were also born there; or give them the right to claim citizenship if they are born in the country and still resident there at majority. Several other countries provide for a right to nationality or give citizenship to children who would otherwise be stateless. Nevertheless, most countries require that at least one parent of a child born on their territory must be a citizen for the child also to be a citizen.

The European models for the laws adopted by independent African states for the most part contained no explicit racial or ethnic component as applied in their metropolitan (as opposed to colonial) territories, and this race and ethnic neutrality is also the majority position in African laws today. Nevertheless, the European-inspired concept of the 'nation-state' – of a state where all the citizens are notionally tied together by a common culture, language and genetic heritage – had a strong influence on new rulers in African countries that for the most part had none of these characteristics. Moreover, the detailed discrimination on the basis of skin colour and ethnicity applied in colonial Africa had been much more widely experienced in practice than the more equal rights that existed in the European states themselves. Especially in those countries most affected by migration during the colonial period, it was tempting to amend the law to exclude those who could not claim to be the authentic owners of the land from time immemorial. Moreover, faced with the challenge of establishing authority over geographical territories of vast cultural diversity that had been created without any regard to pre-existing polities, many African governments treated marginal populations with suspicion, regarding their loyalty as especially suspect when their kith and kin were dominant in a neighbouring state.

According to the particular history of the state in question, laws were thus in many places amended or adapted in practice to exclude those whose ethnic identification with the new state – and in particular with the particular elite who found themselves in power – could be questioned. Thus, for example, the citizenship of white Zimbabweans, Asian Ugandans and Kenyans and Lebanese Sierra Leoneans and others has been explicitly denied, restricted or challenged since independence. A more subtle discrimination against recent arrivals is found in those countries that have citizenship requirements based on the concept of 'indigenous origin'. Even today, the Ugandan and Congolese constitutions provide explicitly that citizenship by birth is restricted to those with a parent from a community indigenous to the country, provisions that still have important effects for the descendants of long-term immigrant populations who have in each generation thus never acquired citizenship by birth. Even where the laws in place are not necessarily problematic, the successive accretions of reform and amendment have in many cases simply made the rules impenetrable even to expert lawyers.

Liberia and Sierra Leone, both founded by freed slaves, have created an emphasis in their citizenship law on authenticity of race rather than indigenous origin: a reverse racial or ethnic discrimination is explicitly written into the law. In Sierra Leone only those 'of negro descent' may be citizens by birth; in the case of Liberia, 'non-negroes' are prohibited from becoming citizens even by naturalization, 'in order to preserve, foster, and maintain the positive Liberian culture, values, and character'. Many other African countries have diluted elements of the same racial preference: in Malawi, citizenship by birth is restricted to those who have at least one parent who is not only a citizen of Malawi but is also 'a person of African race'. Several other countries have a positive spin on the same distinction, giving preferential treatment in terms of naturalization to those who are from another African country (in practice defined in terms of race rather than citizenship). Mali grants citizenship by origin to any child born in Mali of a mother or father 'of African origin' who was himself or herself also born there (but not if neither parent is 'of African origin'). Ghana has recently extended this principle to members of the wider African diaspora, allowing them to settle and ultimately become citizens on easier terms than applied to those not of African descent.

The nervousness over the possible divided loyalties of those with a foot in two countries was reflected in the decision of many

African countries at independence that dual citizenship should not be allowed. Increasingly, however, a post-independence and voluntary African diaspora, in addition to the earlier involuntary diaspora of slavery, has grown to match the European and Asian migrations. These 'hyphenated' Africans with roots both in an African country and a European or American one have brought political pressure to bear on their 'home' governments to change the rules on dual citizenship and concede that someone with two identities need not necessarily be disloyal to either state. In addition, there are increasing numbers of Africans with connections to two African countries – and not only from among ethnic groups found on the borders between two states. A Nigerian-Ghanaian person is as likely a combination as a Nigerian-American or Ghanaian-British. Though a less organized and powerful lobby group, these people too claim an acknowledgement of their multiple identities.

Many African states have thus changed their rules to allow dual citizenship, or are in the process of considering such changes; around half now allow their citizens to hold another passport (though they often retain restrictions on binationals holding senior public office). Angola, Botswana, Burundi, Gabon, Gambia, Ghana, Mozambique, Rwanda, São Tomé and Príncipe, Sierra Leone, South Africa and Uganda have all amended their laws in the last decade or so to allow dual citizenship. Some African countries – notably Ethiopia and Ghana – have created an intermediate status for members of their diasporas, instead of or in addition to creating a right to dual nationality.

As in the European countries that the newly independent countries' citizenship laws were modelled upon, the new laws of many countries in Africa discriminated on the basis of gender. Female citizens were not able to pass on their citizenship to their children if the father was not also a citizen; nor could they pass citizenship to their foreign spouses. (Despite the many indigenous African traditions of belonging and ethnic identity based on matrilineal descent, citizenship discrimination on the continent today is invariably in favour of men.) Thus, in Madagascar, for example, perhaps 5 per cent of the long-established 2-million-strong Muslim community finds itself effectively stateless because complex citizenship rules restrict citizenship by origin to those born of a Malagasy father. There are similar problems in Sierra Leone, Libya, Swaziland and elsewhere.

Since the 1960s, however, the international struggle for women's equality has made strides in Africa as elsewhere, and citizenship law has been among the areas reformed. Today only a few countries still prevent a citizen mother from passing on citizenship to her child if the father is not a citizen. The right of women to pass citizenship to their husbands has proved more of a struggle, though there too the women's movement is making steady gains.

A key moment in this move towards gender equality was the 1993 *Unity Dow* case in Botswana. According to the law in force before the case was brought, Unity Dow, a citizen of Botswana married to an American, was prevented from passing on her Botswanan nationality to her husband and children. The Court of Appeal upheld Dow's victory in the High Court, stating that 'the time that women were treated as chattels or were there to obey the whims and wishes of males is long past and it would be offensive to modern thinking and the spirit of the Constitution to find that the Constitution was deliberately framed to permit discrimination on the ground of sex'. The Citizenship Act was amended to conform with the judgment in 1995, and now allows naturalization of foreign spouses for both men and women, and the acquisition of citizenship by descent if either the father or the mother was a citizen of Botswana at the time of birth.

Since then, perhaps twenty countries have enacted reforms providing for greater (if not in all cases total) gender equality in the right to citizenship, and a majority now do not discriminate on a gender basis in citizenship rights. Yet almost a third of them still discriminate on the grounds of gender in granting citizenship rights to children either when born in their country or born overseas, including Burundi, Guinea, Kenya, Liberia, Libya, Madagascar, Mali, Mauritania, Senegal, Somalia, Sudan, Swaziland, Togo, Tunisia and Zimbabwe. And some relatively recent nationality laws have introduced new discriminatory measures: Swaziland's determinedly backward-looking 2005 law provides that those born after the new law came into force are citizens only if their fathers were citizens.

In addition, more than twenty countries today still do not allow women to pass their citizenship to their non-citizen spouses or apply discriminatory residence qualifications to foreign men married to citizen women who wish to obtain citizenship. The continued resistance to the rights of married women and suspicion of what their spouses may do is reflected in a 2003 African treaty on women's rights. Its provisions do not require states to allow women to pass nationality to their husbands and say only that women and men should have equal rights with respect to the nationality of their children *unless* 'this is contrary to a provision in national legislation or is contrary to national security interests'.[3]

The case of Ethiopia, moreover, illustrates how even when the most important provisions of the law do not apparently discriminate on the face of it, gender discrimination persists in practice. The 1995 Ethiopian constitution is gender neutral in its provision on nationality, and even provides for every child to have the right to a nationality. The 2003 Proclamation on Ethiopian Nationality is also gender neutral, stating that: 'Any person born in Ethiopia or abroad, whose father or mother is Ethiopian, is an Ethiopian subject.' However, the 1930 Ethiopian Nationality Law contained a provision stating that 'Every child born in a lawful mixed marriage follows the nationality of its father.' This is the meaning that is still applied today in practice: the tens if not hundreds of thousands of people who are children of Ethiopian women and foreign men (including Eritreans) are not regarded as Ethiopian in popular understanding and administrative practice even if they were born and have lived all their lives in Ethiopia.

Gender discrimination is particularly problematic in those countries – around half of those in Africa – that make no default provision for children born in the country who would otherwise be stateless to have a right to a nationality, or that provide the 'fall-back' right to a nationality only for children born on the territory with unknown parents (an extremely rare circumstance). This group of people is spread throughout the continent, a vast population of disenfranchised people, excluded from full membership of the country where they live.

3 | Natives and settlers

Since the human species evolved within its boundaries, Africa has seen internal migrations across the vast distances of the continent, as the first peoples travelled in search of new territories and resources and were followed by different population groups over the centuries. For many millennia, Africa's peoples have also left its shores: it is probable that all human beings on the planet are descended from individuals who first came from Africa. North Africa has long exchanged both goods and people with the European countries on the northern side of the Mediterranean Sea. The coastal populations along the countries bordering the Indian Ocean have traded and intermarried with people from the Arabian peninsula and the Indian subcontinent for centuries. The first Europeans arrived in sub-Saharan Africa on voyages of exploration, trade and missionary activity from the end of the fifteenth century, long before the era of military conquest and colonial rule.

The nature of migration slowly changed, however, especially as the European presence in sub-Saharan Africa degenerated into trafficking of human beings followed by colonial conquest. Though a trade in slaves had long existed across the Sahara Desert and the Indian Ocean, the numbers affected dramatically escalated with the Atlantic slave trade, peaking in the late eighteenth century. More than ten million people were ultimately taken from the continent by Europeans, before the abolition of the slave trade in the nineteenth century. No sooner had the slave trade ended than the age of empire began, establishing the foundations of the states we see today. And with empire came further migration: of Europeans to manage the new structures of government and to farm the best land; of other non-Africans as indentured labour to build the new infrastructure or to use that infrastructure for the purposes of trade; and of Africans themselves, either forcibly used as labour on colonial plantations, or following economic opportunities of their own accord.

There are two main groups in Africa today whose members are not themselves migrants but suffer from blanket discrimination in their entitlement to citizenship. The first are the descendants of the more recent immigrant populations (roughly, since the period of nineteenth-century European colonization), including not only Europeans themselves but also those of south Asian descent in east and southern Africa and the 'Lebanese' of west Africa. The second group, most numerous, but least well known, are those of African descent whose ancestral origins lie outside the present borders of the state concerned; and in some cases also their ethnic kin who are not themselves descended from migrants but are lumped together with the more recent arrivals for the purposes of state policy and in popular understanding. Among these are the Banyarwanda of the Democratic Republic of Congo; 'northerners' (as well as descendants of Burkinabé or Malian migrants) in Côte d'Ivoire; and the Nubians of Kenya, black Africans yet still regarded as not eligible for full citizenship because they 'originally' came from somewhere else.

Thus, though it may seem easy to understand a state policy of dispossessing or at least disfavouring those who were previously the dispossessors or who benefited from official favouritism during the period of colonial rule, contemporary policies of dispossession have equally or to a greater extent affected those who were themselves among the victims of empire; or who have been 'guilty' only of migration from another part of Africa in search of economic opportunities.

Although the marginalization of these groups is justified in the official or public mind by their status as newcomers or minorities who do not belong, in practice their status is designated on the basis of race or ethnicity. The number of generations an individual's family has been resident in the territory, fluency in national languages, contribution to economic, political or cultural achievements, and apparent integration into the life of the country may all hold no weight in citizenship regimes that depend in law or practice on proving the absence of an alternative nationality or a line of descent from ancestors who were already in the country at the time of independence.

The case studies below describe the situation of these migrant populations in Zimbabwe, Kenya and Uganda, Sierra Leone, DRC and Côte d'Ivoire. In the last two countries especially, citizenship discrimination has led directly to bloody conflict. As the case of Rwanda shows, discrimination need not be founded on citizenship law to have catastrophic consequences – the 1994 genocide was built on years of systematic government discrimination against one segment of the population, but not in any formal sense on manipulation of the right to be a Rwandan citizen as such – but the denial of citizenship rights has a particular usefulness to governments. If a group of persons are not citizens, then they lose most of the rights to protection that the state should be giving them; they can be argued to be 'outlaws', outside the reach of the law of the place where they live. They enter a world of half-rights and discretionary executive action, free from the supervision of the courts and much of the reach of international law.

Dual citizenship, denationalization and disenfranchisement in Zimbabwe

Zimbabwe provides perhaps the clearest example of policies of dispossession dating from the era of colonial and minority rule returning boomerang-like to give their perpetrators' descendants a knock-out blow. Yet those worst affected by the efforts to denationalize the 'former oppressors' have not been white Zimbabweans but rather the African migrants from neighbouring countries who have travelled to Zimbabwe in search of economic opportunities.

What was then Rhodesia was one of the most favoured destinations for white settlement under the British empire. Profitable commercial farms were rapidly established on the rich land expropriated from its former cultivators, and the colonial government established systems to recruit cheap labour from neighbouring Nyasaland (today's Malawi), Northern Rhodesia (Zambia) and Mozambique. Though new foreign recruitment largely ceased with the unilateral declaration of independence from Britain in 1965, the existing farm workers remained, and by the 1980s between a quarter and a half of farm workers were still of foreign origin (though the vast majority had been born in Zimbabwe). An end to white minority rule came in 1980 after a protracted war of liberation, but was ultimately negotiated through talks brokered by the British government that established a new government elected on the basis of universal suffrage and headed by Robert Mugabe (first as prime minister and from 1987 as president), the leader of the dominant liberation movement, the Zimbabwe African National Union – Patriotic Front (ZANU-PF).

The twists and turns of Zimbabwe's citizenship law since majority rule was attained shadow the political history of the country. Over the years, a law that at first glance appears to provide for a *jus soli* right to citizenship for all individuals born in the country has become so bound about with exceptions based on foreign parentage and gender bias that it is virtually impossible for the non-lawyer to decide whether someone is indeed a citizen. Adding to the complications are the ever-stricter rules that have been applied relating to those Zimbabweans who might have a possible claim on some other citizenship – whether or not they actually hold that citizenship in fact. Whereas many other African countries have gradually relaxed their rules on dual nationality, Zimbabwe has moved so far in the opposite direction that it can in fact be impossible for someone descended from immigrants to the country to be a citizen.

The first version of Zimbabwe's constitution, negotiated under restrictive conditions and British supervision, allowed dual citizenship. As in the case of constitutional provisions providing special protections for white Zimbabweans and res-tricting redistribution of land for the first decade of majority rule, this provision was opposed by ZANU-PF. Unlike the other transitional arrangements, permission to hold dual nationality had no special protection. ZANU-PF moved quickly to address this question: in 1983, the constitution was amended to prohibit dual citizenship.[1]

A new citizenship law passed in 1984 confirmed this position and also introduced a requirement that Zimbabwean citizens with an entitlement to another citizenship renounce that right by the end of 1985.[2] This provision was directed primarily at those white Zimbabweans with a British or other passport, or the right to another passport. Though perhaps two-thirds of the up to a quarter-million white Zimbabweans left the country during the years immediately after independence, tens of thousands did renounce their entitlement to a foreign citizenship before Zimbabwean officials and kept or obtained Zimbabwean passports as a result; thousands more remained in the country as permanent residents but used foreign passports.

When dual citizenship was abolished, however, many persons of foreign origin with less access to information than the white population typically had – especially farm workers – were deprived of their Zimbabwean citizenship because they had failed to sign the prescribed form renouncing their foreign citizenship. In 1990, the government provided a partial response to the excluded status of this group by adding a new provision to the constitution that extended the categories of voters entitled to vote in a presidential or parliamentary election beyond citizens to 'persons who, since 31 December 1985, have been regarded by virtue of a written law as permanently resident in Zimbabwe'.[3] Thus, the government ensured they were not deprived of the franchise as well as their citizenship – no doubt with the hope of obtaining their votes in return. Yet farm workers were still regarded with suspicion by the government, tainted by their association with white farm owners even though they were among the lowest-paid groups in Zimbabwe.

Running in parallel with this racially charged debate on dual nationality was a separate – but related – argument over gender discrimination. Under Zimbabwean citizenship law, women do not have the right to pass on citizenship to their non-Zimbabwean

41

husbands, nor to their children by a non-Zimbabwean father. Immigration law also subjected foreign husbands (but not wives) of Zimbabwean citizens to the discretion of the state in terms of their right to reside in Zimbabwe. In 1994, the Supreme Court of Zimbabwe ruled that these restrictions violated the constitutional right of Zimbabwean women to freedom of movement.[4] The government promptly introduced a bill to amend the constitution to enable the restrictions on foreign husbands to be reinstated. Just as in the case of dual citizenship, although the amendment was presented as a law that would only affect 'elite' women bringing husbands from overseas, most of those potentially affected were rural women living in Zimbabwe's border regions. Women's rights activists won a pyrrhic victory over the bill: the government conceded on the gender discrimination point, but the constitutional amendment was resubmitted and passed in a form that ensured that restrictions on freedom of movement could be applied to foreign wives as well as husbands of Zimbabwean citizens.

In 1999, a new opposition movement was formed in Zimbabwe, the Movement for Democratic Change (MDC), to contest upcoming elections and challenge the long dominance of ZANU-PF. The MDC campaigned against a proposed new constitution put forward by the government, which had co-opted a citizens' movement for constitutional reform by creating a ZANU-PF-dominated constitutional commission to draft a new text. The draft constitution, which would have greatly strengthened the executive at the expense of parliament as well as extending the powers of the government to acquire land compulsorily without compensation, was rejected in a February 2000 referendum. In June 2000, parliamentary elections were held. The MDC won fifty-seven seats, only just short of the sixty-two seats won by ZANU-PF, and took 77 per cent of the urban vote. ZANU-PF chose to attribute its losses to the MDC in the referendum and elections to the influence and finance of white Zimbabwean citizens considered anti-government, especially the approximately four thousand white commercial farm owners, as well as the by now several hundred thousand farm workers and their families. In addition to mobilizing violence against the opposition and other measures, steps were taken to amend the criteria for Zimbabwean citizenship, with the transparent aim of disenfranchising these groups.

In May 2000, the government warned whites they would be stripped of their Zimbabwe citizenship if they could not produce foreign documentation showing they had no entitlement to the citizenship of another country. Around 86,000 whites who had allegedly failed to renounce their British citizenship would have to turn in their Zimbabwean passports, a government newspaper advertisement stated; of these, around 30,000 were adults, able to vote.[5] In accordance with this announcement, the registrar-general's office[6] began to refuse to renew the Zimbabwean passports of many whites, arguing they should have renounced any entitlement to foreign nationality to individual foreign governments.

At least two court cases successfully challenged these provisions. In December 2000, the Supreme Court ruled against the registrar-general, in a case brought by Robyn Carr, a businesswoman whose application to renew her passport had been refused by the registrar-general on the grounds that she must prove she had renounced her British citizenship under British law. But the Supreme Court ordered renewal because she had complied with the requirements of renunciation under Zimbabwean law by filling in a form of renunciation of citizenship, and the registrar-general had no power to require her to renounce her citizenship under British law.[7] In January 2001, Sterling Purser, an eighteen-year-old born in Harare in 1982 of a British father, was denied a passport on the grounds that he had not renounced his British citizenship. Purser challenged the decision, arguing that he had fulfilled the legal requirements to renounce his entitlement to foreign citizenship, and the Supreme Court agreed, following its earlier ruling in the Carr case. In both cases, the Supreme Court awarded costs against the registrar-general.[8]

In light of these court defeats and the electoral results of 2000, the government introduced the Citizenship Amendment

Act No. 12 of 2001, which strengthened the provisions for renunciation drastically, including inserting a provision requiring
renunciation under the relevant foreign law, and not only under
Zimbabwean law:[9] Section 9(7) provided that:

> A citizen of Zimbabwe of full age who –
>
> a) at the date of commencement of the Citizenship Amendment
> Act, 2001, is also a citizen of a foreign country; or
>
> b) at any time before that date, had renounced or purported to
> renounce his citizenship of a foreign country and has, despite
> such renunciation, retained his citizenship of that country;
> shall cease to be a citizen of Zimbabwe six months after that
> date unless, before the expiry of that period, he has effectively
> renounced his foreign citizenship in accordance with the law
> of that foreign country and has made a declaration confirming
> such renunciation in the form and manner prescribed.

According to the state-owned media, quoting a government official, the amendment was required because '[t]here are concerns
that those with dual citizenship are behind efforts to discredit
the Government economically and politically by enlisting foreign
governments to use diplomatic and other means to topple the
ZANU-PF Government'.[10] Information Minister Jonathan Moyo
described passports as 'privileges' not rights, and threatened
their withdrawal from anyone involved in calls for international
sanctions against Zimbabwe.[11]

While lawyers argued that the amendment act required only
those people who actually had dual citizenship to renounce
their foreign citizenship according to the laws of their respective countries, the law was applied more expansively. Registrar-
General Tobaiwa Mudede placed an advertisement in a national
newspaper stating that even those people with only a claim to
foreign citizenship (but no citizenship in fact) had to renounce
that potential citizenship. He repeatedly restated this position.
Thus, for example, a person born in Zimbabwe of a father of
Malawian descent and a mother of Mozambican origin had to

renounce entitlement to Malawian and Mozambican citizenship: something virtually impossible to do. Despite protests from farm workers' organizations at this interpretation of the act, the registrar-general issued a statement confirming that 'any failure by farm workers to renounce foreign citizenship in the form and manner prescribed by the foreign law will result in loss of Zimbabwean citizenship after 6th January 2002'.[12] Before the 6 January deadline, the Mozambican high commission in Harare stated that it was overwhelmed with applications for documentary proof that persons of Mozambican descent were not eligible for Mozambican citizenship, and were unable to supply it.[13]

As Mudede confirmed, the vast majority of persons affected by the amendment were farm workers and others born in neighbouring countries or whose parents were born in neighbouring countries.[14] But although the amendment was given some publicity in the urban areas of Zimbabwe, many affected citizens in the outlying areas remained uninformed until the deadline set had passed and their Zimbabwean citizenship had been lost by operation of law.

A class action suit challenging the registrar-general's interpretation of the citizenship law was filed with the High Court in October 2001 by Lesley Leventhe Petho. Although it was initially struck out by the High Court, on the grounds that Petho's case was not sufficiently typical to be the basis of a class action (he was born in Zimbabwe, the son of Hungarians who had fled the aftermath of the 1956 uprising), the Supreme Court confirmed the possibility of bringing a class action case in October 2002, providing Petho advertised in national newspapers and on radio to let others in the same plight know he was doing this.[15] The state-run Zimbabwe Broadcasting Corporation then refused to accept his advertisements, and negotiations to have the advertisements run at an affordable price never reached conclusion.

Several other cases were successfully brought in the High Court over the next year. In February 2002, the High Court ruled in a case brought by trade union and opposition leader Morgan Tsvangirai, stating that it could not be assumed that a person had a right to foreign citizenship only because his parents were born elsewhere and that a person could not be required to renounce what they had never possessed, and extending the deadline for renunciations to 6 August 2002.[16] In May 2002, the High Court found in favour of Judith Todd, daughter of former Rhodesian prime minister Sir Garfield Todd, deposed as head of government when he tried to liberalize Rhodesia's apartheid-style rule, and herself a high-profile opponent of the former white minority regime. In 1998, she had become a shareholder and director of Associated Newspapers of Zimbabwe, publisher of the newly established independent newspaper the *Daily News*. The registrar-general asserted that Judith Todd should lose her citizenship because she had not renounced any claim to citizenship of New Zealand, where her father was born. The court, however, ruled that she was still a Zimbabwean citizen, and ordered the restoration of her passport.[17] She was issued a temporary passport, valid for one year, and the government appealed. In June 2002, the High Court also ruled in favour of Ricarudo Manwere, a well-known Zimbabwean dancer of Mozambican parentage.[18]

Presidential elections were held in March 2002. In January, the first set of 'notices of objection' issued in terms of section 25 of the Electoral Act were sent to Zimbabwean citizens who had purportedly lost their Zimbabwean citizenship because they had failed to comply with the terms of the Citizenship Amendment Act No. 12 of 2001. Each notice alleged that the person affected had lost his/her Zimbabwean citizenship and therefore was no longer entitled to remain on the voters' roll. The affected voter was given seven days to appeal to the constituency registrar. There were two distinct groups of people who received notices in error: those who had in fact renounced their foreign citizenship and thus remained Zimbabwean citizens, and those who had never been Zimbabwean citizens and had always been entitled to vote as permanent residents since 31 December 1985; and a further disputed group who had failed to renounce a potential right to foreign citizenship. In a large majority of the cases the notices were received after the seven-day deadline, and when individuals attempted to lodge their appeals they met with resistance and refusal by the constituency registrar and the registrar-general's office. Many affected farm labourers and rural dwellers never in fact received these notices, and were summarily struck off the voters' roll without first having had an opportunity to be heard.

In parallel with the cases dealing with dual citizenship, the issue of the rights of permanent residents under the constitutional provision allowing both citizens and permanent residents to vote also came into dispute in the courts. Lawyers argued that those who had supposedly lost their Zimbabwean citizenship under the new rules were nevertheless entitled to be on the voters' roll and vote, because they remained permanent residents. In January 2002, in another case brought by Morgan Tsvangirai, the High Court ordered the registrar-general to restore this group of persons to the voters' roll.[19] In February, however, the Supreme Court overturned this decision, holding that citizens and permanent residents were two separate statuses that could not be held at the same time, and those who had lost their citizenship were therefore not permanent residents by default and not entitled to vote.[20] Other cases in the High Court followed the Supreme Court's ruling.[21] Litigation on these issues was still under way as the presidential election was held on 9–11 March, including a challenge to a new statutory instrument issued on 9 March that changed the rules for disputes over the voters' roll. On the days of polling those people who had obtained orders from the magistrates' courts in favour of their right to be on the voters' roll were none the less denied the chance to vote.

In 2005, the government ended this argument, by passing the Constitution of Zimbabwe Amendment (No. 17) Act. Among many sections dealing with land ownership and the creation of a second chamber in the national parliament, the act also repealed the constitutional provision allowing adults with permanent residency in Zimbabwe to vote.[22] (The same act also amended the section of the constitution dealing with freedom of movement to allow restrictions on movement imposed 'in the national interest, or in the interests of defence, public safety, public order, public morality, public health, the public interest or the economic interests of the State'. That is, it allowed the government to seize passports and stop MDC representatives or civil society activists from travelling outside Zimbabwe.)

Among those disenfranchised by the various legislative amendments was Sir Garfield Todd, who had, somewhat ironically, previously been deprived of his passport by the government of the last Rhodesian prime minister, Ian Smith. In addition to having his citizenship revoked when the new rules came into force, Garfield Todd's name was put on a list of those not allowed to vote supplied by Registrar-General Mudede to all polling stations, even if, like his, their names were actually printed on the current voters' roll. Aged ninety-four, he still attempted to vote, and was refused.[23] Paying attention to symmetry, the government also refused to renew the passport of Ian Smith.[24]

In November 2002, the minister of justice published a cabinet-approved notice in the *Government Gazette* clarifying that renunciation of citizenship would not apply to a potential right to foreign citizenship, but only to a person who was actually and presently a citizen of a foreign country.[25] (In June 2007, a parliamentary committee of which MDC members formed a substantial part issued a report supporting the cabinet's 2002 notice, to no effect.[26])

Despite this, the registrar-general continued to apply the rule that renunciation applied to potential as well as actual citizenship. Moreover, in February 2003, the Supreme Court – which by 2002 had been augmented by judges known to support the government – considered the government's appeal against the ruling in Judith Todd's case and agreed with the government's interpretation that a potential claim to citizenship had to be renounced, as well as an actual citizenship. It examined New Zealand law and concluded that although Judith Todd had not actively sought New Zealand citizenship at any time in her life, she was nevertheless entitled to it under the foreign law, and therefore should renounce such entitlement. If she did not do so within two days, she would lose Zimbabwean citizenship.[27] Todd attempted to comply with the ruling. The New Zealand authorities, however, responded in July, stating that they had received Todd's application for renunciation of citizenship, but that this application could not be processed as she had never laid claim to New Zealand citizenship.

The High Court, however, the first to hear these cases, continued to rule against the registrar-general on the grounds that individuals had in fact no foreign citizenship to renounce. In June 2005, the High Court handed down a judgment in favour of lawyer Job Sibanda, whose father was born in Malawi, finding that Sibanda was 'a Zimbabwean citizen with all privileges, duties and obligations attaching such citizenship'.[28] In 2006, yet another High Court case confirmed the right of lawyer Lewis Uriri, born in Zimbabwe of Mozambican parents, to obtain a birth certificate for his son.[29] In January 2007, the High Court ordered the registrar-general to issue a passport to Trevor Ncube, owner of the independent and critical newspapers the *Zimbabwe Independent* and the *Standard*, who had been informed in December 2005 that he had forfeited his Zimbabwean citizenship because he had failed to renounce his Zambian citizenship (his father was born in Zambia).[30] Ncube's passport was restored to him.

Protests from the southern African region about the Zimbabwe government's treatment of those whose parents had origins in neighbouring countries did eventually lead to a concession in favour specifically of migrant workers from Southern African Development Community (SADC) countries. In 2003 the Citizenship of Zimbabwe Act was amended to allow people who were born in a SADC country, but whose parents came to Zimbabwe as farm labourers, mineworkers, domestic employees or 'in any other unskilled occupation', to apply for 'confirmation' of their citizenship of Zimbabwe and at the same time sign a form renouncing their foreign citizenship (without the need to obtain any documentation from the other SADC country).[31] Although this should have substantially improved the situation of the many farm workers who had been rendered stateless, the amendment was published after most of the people concerned had already lost their Zimbabwean citizenship, and did not have retroactive effect.

In 2007, the Zimbabwe government introduced a bill to parliament to support the 'economic empowerment of indigenous Zimbabweans'. Indigenous Zimbabweans were defined in the bill as 'any person who before the 18th April 1980 was disadvantaged by unfair discrimination on the grounds of his or her race, and any descendant of such person, and includes any company, association, syndicate or partnership of which indigenous Zimbabweans form the majority of the members or hold the controlling interest'.[32] The law, which was adopted unchanged, required that at least 51 per cent of all companies, publicly quoted or private, should be held by indigenous Zimbabweans, and established other procedures for ensuring their economic empowerment.

Throughout the ever-increasing insistence on pure Zimbabwean ancestry for those wishing to claim Zimbabwean citizenship, the government has taken care to give the appearance of respect for a rule of law by adopting statutes and constitutional amendments in the usual legalistic terms. Yet the effect has been to overturn the legal conventions and principles that are the basis of international human rights law, including as it applies to nationality. Because many of the most high-profile figures affected by citizenship discrimination have been white Zimbabweans and because the citizenship issue has been tied to land redistribution, the Zimbabwean government has been able to gain a measure of support from across Africa, even though the most numerous victims of the policy are black Africans from neighbouring countries. Yet the perverted rules of nationality that Zimbabwe has sought to apply have transparently been adopted for political purposes to silence critics and divert attention from the real issues. The consequences of such misguided and unjust policies for all Zimbabweans, most of all the poorest, have become ever more apparent the longer they have remained in effect.

Ethnic exclusion in Kenya and Uganda

In the east African countries of Kenya and Uganda, unlike in Zimbabwe, the great majority of those whites who had acquired land and property during the period of British colonial rule left at independence. Though vast white-owned estates still exist in Kenya, they are few, and the resentment that they might perhaps have generated against whites in the post-independence era has instead been targeted at the south Asian migrants who migrated at a time when both east Africa and the Indian subcontinent were equally part of the British Empire. Asians for the most part did not acquire large landed estates, but they did achieve an economic success that came to be seen to pose a threat to the autonomy of the new states. To undercut the political power that relative wealth might have given them, the new states argued that these Asian immigrants should not have the right to be full citizens – and then took action accordingly.

Asian migration to east Africa began many centuries ago, as trading links across the Indian Ocean were developed among coastal communities in what are now Somalia, Kenya, Tanzania, Mozambique, Yemen, Oman, the Gulf States, Pakistan, India, and farther afield. This contact was accelerated and brought into the interior of the continent under British colonial rule, especially in Kenya and Uganda, where thousands of people from the Indian subcontinent were either imported to work as indentured labour on the railways, or came as traders and businessmen following the economic opportunities those railways brought.

In both Kenya and Uganda, the status of the newer populations of south Asian descent, by then numbering around 175,000 (the majority in Kenya), was highly sensitive during the period leading up to and immediately after independence. In particular, the criteria for acquiring citizenship by registration – an easier process than citizenship by naturalization, and intended to cater for the descendants of Asian or European immigrants – became a subject of debate and dispute, especially in Uganda.

The constitutions of both Kenya and Uganda applied the same rules for acquiring citizenship at independence: a person who was born in Kenya or Uganda of at least one parent who was also born in the country, and who was on the date of independence a citizen of the United Kingdom and colonies or a British protected

51

person, automatically became a citizen of the newly independent country.[33] In addition, a person born outside the country was automatically a citizen if his father became a citizen according to these rules. Various categories of people with a connection to the country had the right to apply for citizenship by registration, including those caught by the exception for those whose parents were born outside the country, as well as those who had married a citizen. These provisions enabled white settlers, Asians and others of non-Kenyan or Ugandan origin to become citizens of the two countries. The constitutions also recognized Commonwealth citizens as a special category of people, but prohibited dual citizenship for adults.[34] Other non-citizens would follow the process of naturalization, with different conditions.

Both during the independence negotiations and immediately after the adoption of the new constitutions, discontent over the economically advantaged position of Asian immigrants to Kenya and Uganda led to agitation for changes in the law. In both countries, citizenship law was modified and restrictions placed on the business operations of 'non-indigenous' populations; in Uganda, these changes were far more radical, and eventually led to the expulsion of the population of Asian descent.[35]

The 1963 Kenya Citizenship Act (revised in 1988) basically reiterated the constitutional provisions with regard to citizenship. Section 92, however, on registration of citizens, introduced a requirement not present in the constitution that an applicant to be registered as a citizen had to satisfy the minister that he was of 'African descent'. In addition, the person had to show either that 'he was born, and one of his parents was born, in a country to which this section applies'; or that 'he has been resident for a period of not less than ten years in a country to which this section applies and he is not a citizen of an independent state on the Continent of Africa'.[36] The minister could declare the countries to which the section applied (essentially on the basis of reciprocity). This provision was rooted in a commitment to African solidarity, in an era before all African states were independent; it has, however, been little used, if at all.[37]

In Uganda, the requirements of the 1962 independence constitution were implemented by the Uganda Citizenship Ordinance.[38] The ordinance provided that Commonwealth citizens or British protected persons (including most whites and Asians) could register as citizens if they applied before 9 October 1964, and satisfied the minister that they had been resident for five years, among other conditions. The 1962 constitution and the Citizenship Ordinance also gave the minister extensive powers to revoke citizenship granted in this way. During the parliamentary proceedings, Asian members of parliament argued unsuccessfully for an easier application and registration process and a more stringent process for revoking citizenship. By 1967, only 11,000 of the 25,000 applicants for registration had been granted citizenship.

The question of citizenship for Asians living in Uganda after independence continued in the 1967 constitutional debate, and slightly more generous provisions were made, by adding the right to derive citizenship from a grandparent and removing gender discrimination. In addition to recognizing existing citizens and new registrations, the 1967 constitution provided citizenship for those born after the constitution came into force to people born in or outside of Uganda with a citizen parent or grandparent.[39]

Both Uganda and Kenya also took measures to promote the 'Africanization' of the economy, perceived to be too dominated by businesses owned by Kenyans of European and Asian descent. Each country passed a Trade Licensing Act, in 1969 and 1977 respectively, to restrict the operations of non-African-owned businesses.

In Kenya, these measures led to a case before the Kenyan High Court in 1968 which considered the concept of 'African descent' under the Citizenship Act in order to decide whether non-Africans could be deprived of property rights.[40] The plaintiffs were individuals of Asian descent who had been given notices to quit the stalls they rented from Nairobi city council following a resolution on the Africanization of commerce. They had been born in Kenya but did not qualify automatically for citizenship because their parents had not been born in the country, though they were entitled to and had applied for citizenship by registration and were awaiting the results. The court found that the implementation of the resolution was discriminatory in practice and that the quit notices were void – but not that the policy or the resolution were unconstitutional in themselves, on the grounds that the constitutional protection against discrimination did not apply to non-citizens.[41] Effectively, the court accepted that the state's delay in processing applications for citizenship justified its actions against the very same group of people.

In Uganda, these measures went much farther following the takeover of power in 1971 by President Idi Amin, who sought to return the Asian-controlled businesses to 'black Ugandans', on the grounds that the Asians were 'sabotaging Uganda's economy and encouraging corruption'.[42] On 4 August 1972, he announced that he would demand that the British government take over responsibility for the 80,000 Asian British passport holders in Uganda and ensure their removal from Uganda within three months. Successive decrees cancelled all entry permits and certificates of residence issued to persons of Asian origin, and had a knock-on effect on other foreigners, most of whom left the country.[43]

In 1983 the new government reversed these policies, passing legislation to return confiscated property and encouraging the return of the Asian community and other foreigners and investors to Uganda[44] – though the process was not a simple one and there was much controversy over ownership of the property formerly held by Asians.[45]

In 1995, a new constitution was promulgated in Uganda following a countrywide consultative process led by a constitutional review commission (known as the Odoki Commission, after its chair). While the status of those of Asian descent had dominated the drafting of the 1962 and 1967 constitutions, the 1994/95 constitutional debate focused on the status of African immigrants and refugees. In particular, because of the controversial status of the 'Rwandese Tutsi' who had come to Uganda as refugees,

many Ugandans opposed the recognition of 'Banyarwanda' as
citizens. Though a minority sought a more restrictive position,
however, many Ugandans wanted citizenship to be defined to
include all people who had been in Uganda for a long period
of time and wished to obtain citizenship.[47]

The 1995 constitution introduced an explicit ethnic definition
of Ugandan citizenship for the first time. It provides for a right
to citizenship by birth for two categories: first, for every person
born in Uganda, 'one of whose parents or grandparents is or
was a member of any of the indigenous communities existing
and residing within the borders of Uganda as at the first day of
February, 1926'; and second, for every person born in or outside

Uganda one of whose parents or grandparents was a citizen of Uganda by birth.[48] Both categories, the former explicitly, the latter by implication, privilege the ethnic groups historically resident in Uganda, making it difficult for whites and Asians to obtain Ugandan nationality. A schedule listing the 'indigenous communities' of Uganda generated some of the hottest debate as the constitution was adopted; Asians argued unsuccessfully that they should be regarded as an indigenous group. Fifty-six groups were eventually included, among them the Banyarwanda, as well as other cross-border ethnic groups such as the Batwa, Lendu and Karamojong; in 2005, a further nine were added to the list.[49] Uganda thus joined the small group of countries that make it effectively impossible for those of the 'wrong' race or ethnicity to become citizens with full rights, a choice that may well have long-term consequences for its stability.[50]

The 'Lebanese' of Sierra Leone

In west Africa, migration from south Asia was less common than in the countries that came to make up the East African Community. As in east Africa, the laws governing the transition to independence were non-discriminatory on a racial or ethnic basis; but very similar sorts of discrimination in law and practice have since independence been adopted in several countries against the Middle Eastern migrants who came to the region under colonial rule. Among the more extreme cases are the two west African neighbouring countries where freed slaves played the leading role in the early years of self-government: Liberia and Sierra Leone. In each case, the history of oppression by white people and favoured immigrants from other continents led to the adoption of laws that excluded those not of African descent from full membership of the new states. In Liberia, the constitution has, since the first version was adopted in 1847, always provided that only a 'Negro' may be a citizen, whatever the other circumstances (though a single great-grandparent who was fully black may be enough to call an individual 'Negro').[51] Sierra Leone applies a similar rule: though it allows non-blacks to naturalize, it makes this extremely difficult in practice, and citizenship by birth is restricted to 'Negro Africans', defined – until 2006 – with reference to the male line only.

The kernel for the British colony of Sierra Leone was founded in 1787, when several hundred immigrants, made up largely but not only of London's 'poor blacks' supported by funds from the abolitionist movement, arrived in the territory and established the first new settlement. In 1792, bolstered by the arrival of ex-slaves from Nova Scotia, the settlers established Freetown, and were joined there by other 'returnees' from Jamaica and America. Then, from the date of the abolition of the slave trade by the British parliament in 1807, the British navy began intercepting slave ships travelling from Africa to the Americas, and landed thousands of freed slaves in Freetown, where a naval base had been established. The colony previously managed by the private Sierra Leone Company was surrendered to the British crown in the same year. Though contacts both peaceful and military between the colony and the interior then steadily increased, it was not until 1896 that a British Protectorate was declared over the full territory of what is now Sierra Leone.

During the late nineteenth century, migrants from what are now Syria and Lebanon but was then the Ottoman Empire began arriving in Freetown, which had become a thriving port, and set up businesses as traders. Lebanese nationals also came to settle in Sierra Leone much more recently, especially during the civil war in Lebanon. Something less than 1 per cent of Sierra Leone's estimated 5–6 million population was at one time made up of individuals of Middle Eastern descent, known collectively as 'Lebanese'; though the numbers diminished greatly during the civil war to perhaps fewer than ten thousand. Many of these 'Lebanese' have parents and grandparents born in Sierra Leone, speak Sierra Leonean languages, and have intermarried and actively participated in the political, social and economic life of the country. At the same time, a strong Lebanese identity is retained by some, through institutions such as the Lebanese International School in Freetown, which teaches the Arabic language and Lebanese history, as well as the history and curriculum for Sierra Leone. Some have retained Lebanese passports. The Lebanese in Sierra Leone, as elsewhere in west Africa, are for the most part business people, dominating commerce in the large towns.

In 1961, the independence constitution of Sierra Leone created a single nationality, without any distinction by race, ethnic group or sex. 'Every person' born in the former colony or protectorate who was a citizen of the United Kingdom and colonies or a British protected person on 26 April 1961 became a citizen of Sierra Leone on 27 April 1961, unless neither of his or her parents nor any of his or her grandparents was born in Sierra Leone.[52] The 1961 constitution also had an extensive bill of rights guaranteeing the protection of the rights of all individuals without discrimination. Thus, the small population of 'Lebanese' and the offspring of interracial marriages were all recognized as citizens of Sierra Leone.

Within a year after independence, Sierra Leone's constitutional provisions on citizenship were amended twice to become more restrictive and discriminate against individuals on the basis of race, colour and sex.[53] First, the words 'of negro African descent' were inserted immediately after the words 'every person', to apply retroactively from the date of independence. Then the non-discrimination clause that prohibited any law that is 'discriminatory of itself or in its effect' was amended to exclude laws relating to citizenship. Individuals who were not of 'negro African descent' but who had acquired citizenship by virtue of the 1961 constitution were thus stripped of their citizenship of Sierra Leone after less than a year. (In Britain, meanwhile, the 1962 Commonwealth Immigrants Act introduced for the first time restrictions on immigration to Britain for citizens of former colonies. Though not explicitly racial in its language, the new provisions were aimed at non-white immigrants from the newly independent countries of Africa and the Caribbean; the effect was to leave some residents of former British colonies with no right of citizenship in any country.)

The 1962 constitutional amendments defined 'person of negro African descent' as follows: 'a person whose father and his father's father are or were negroes of African origin', introducing both racial and gender discrimination at one step. Even if a person was born in Sierra Leone of a 'negro African' mother, that person could not qualify for citizenship by birth if that person's father or grandfather was not of negro African descent. The amendments also provided that a person whose mother (but not father or grandfather) was a negro of African descent could apply to be registered as a citizen. A registered citizen did not, however, qualify to become a member of the 'House of Representatives, or of any District Council or other local authority unless he shall have resided continuously in Sierra Leone for twenty-five years after such registration or shall have served in the civil or regular Armed Services of Sierra Leone for a continuous period of twenty-five years'.[54] Nor did the law stipulate how registration should be undertaken.

The change to the law was motivated by political considerations; in particular, to narrow the set of candidates eligible to contest elections due to be held in 1962, by depriving Lebanese and mixed-race Sierra Leoneans of the political rights conferred by citizenship. Subsequent laws restricted the rights of non-citizens to acquire property both in the Western Area (the historic colony, near Freetown) and in the provinces (though it did not take any right away from those non-citizens who had already purchased property in the Western Area).[55] From 1965, the government introduced successive acts restricting non-citizens' ability to own and profit from retail trade, and promoting citizen participation in commerce. In 1969 a new government introduced a further trade act that widened the scope of restrictions, barring non-citizens from trading in thirty-eight consumer goods, rather than the eight previously listed, except by special licence from the minister. The restrictions were also extended to other Africans resident in Sierra Leone, and not just those from overseas; affecting in particular the large community of Fula traders, many originating from neighbouring Guinea.[56] Another act required all non-citizens to register their presence, and gave the government extensive powers to expel non-citizens in the interests of the 'public good'.[57]

These legal changes took place against a turbulent political background. In 1964, Sir Milton Margai, leader of the Sierra Leone People's Party (SLPP) and the new state's first prime minister, died and was succeeded by his brother, Sir Albert Margai. In closely contested elections in March 1967, Siaka Stevens, candidate of the All People's Congress (APC), was declared winner over Margai – only to be ousted in a coup within a few hours. A year of military rule by successive groups was ended with a return to civilian rule in 1968 under Siaka Stevens. Though further disturbances and attempted coups followed, Stevens retained power for the next seventeen years, first as prime minister and then, after a republican constitution was adopted in 1971, as president.

John Joseph Akar, a prominent mixed-race Sierra Leonean with political ambitions, became the best-known case of those affected by the changes to citizenship law and the face of efforts to reverse them. Akar's mother was a black Sierra Leonean; his father was of Lebanese origin and thus not 'of negro African descent', though he had never visited Lebanon. When Sierra Leone became independent on 27 April 1961, Akar automatically became a citizen by operation of the constitution, as both he and one of his parents had been born in Sierra Leone. With the 1962 amendments, however, he lost his citizenship by birth; though he did apply for and was granted citizenship by registration. He challenged the amendments in court. In his application, he contended that the true intention of the amendments was to exclude persons not of 'negro African descent' from being elected to the House of Representatives. He succeeded in the High Court, but the Court of Appeal subsequently reversed the decision. Akar appealed to the Privy Council in England (then the highest court for Sierra Leone). In 1969 the Privy Council reversed the Court of Appeal decision and declared that the amendment was of no effect, though on different grounds from the judge at first instance.[58]

The victory was short lived. The Siaka Stevens government

disregarded the judgment and re-enacted the discriminatory provisions in the Sierra Leone Citizenship Act 1973.[59] The government also established its own Supreme Court in Sierra Leone, removing the right of appeal to the Privy Council.

The 1973 Citizenship Act provided for two categories of citizenship: by birth and by naturalization. Citizenship by birth was granted to anyone born in Sierra Leone before 19 April 1971, or resident in Sierra Leone on 18 April 1971, provided that his or her father or grandfather was born in Sierra Leone and that he or she 'is person of negro African descent'. Dual citizenship was excluded. Persons entitled to apply for naturalization under the 1973 Act were foreign women married to citizens, other persons of 'negro African descent' born in Sierra Leone, and persons of 'negro African descent' continuously resident for a period of not less than eight years.[60] Persons who were Afro-Lebanese (i.e. those whose mothers were black Sierra Leonean and whose fathers were not 'negro' African) could apply to be naturalized under this provision (though no procedures to do so were established). The 1973 Act does not define who is a 'negro African', and the 1962 amendment had also provided little clarity. The presumption was that the phrase meant black African, reducing the essential condition for the acquisition of citizenship to the colour of the person's skin. Thus a black man's children by a Sierra Leonean black woman were citizens by birth wherever they were born. A white or mixed-race man's children by a Sierra Leonean woman could acquire Sierra Leonean citizenship only by naturalization. The 1983 Births and Deaths Registration Act reinforced this discrimination by requiring the officer registering a child's birth to include the race of the child's parents in the birth certificate.[61]

Those without a parent of 'negro African descent' did not even have a right to naturalize until an amendment to the Citizenship Act came into force in 1977, allowing for individuals over twenty-one years of age and without a parent of 'negro African descent' to apply for naturalization based on a residence period of fifteen years and other restrictive criteria.[62] Those under twenty-one could apply to naturalize only if one of their parents was already naturalized. Persons of 'negro African descent' born in Sierra Leone could apply for naturalization at any time, with no further requirements; and those with a parent of 'negro African descent' not born in the country could apply for naturalization after only eight years. The minister was not required to give any reason for the refusal of any application for naturalization and his decision on any such application could not be challenged in any court.[63] The minister also had very wide powers to revoke the grant of citizenship by naturalization. A person whose certificate is revoked ceases to be a Sierra Leonean and may be subject to expulsion.[64] Moreover, dual citizenship was forbidden. In practice, naturalization became progressively more difficult to obtain, except by payment of a bribe.

The Citizenship Act was further amended in 1976 to exclude naturalized persons from holding a wider range of public offices.[65] After a period of twenty-five years, the restrictions could be lifted; but only by parliamentary resolution passed by a two-thirds majority. In 1978, a referendum approved a new constitution that confirmed the discriminatory provisions in relation to citizenship while making the country a one-party state. Despite these restrictions, Lebanese commercial interests were central to the increasing corruption and 'privatization' of the Sierra Leonean state under the Stevens government, and especially to the exploitation of Sierra Leone's important alluvial diamond industry. The trade acts were used rather as a source of revenue for the government than to restrict non-citizens' ability to operate businesses in practice.

Siaka Stevens retired from office in 1985, and installed Joseph Saidu Momoh as his successor. Pulled by the tide of reform that swept across Africa with the end of the cold war, Momoh instituted a constitutional review process. A new constitution was adopted in 1991 that provided for multiparty elections but did not address the citizenship questions, endorsing the discrimination established in the citizenship acts.[66]

In March 1991, fighters from a group calling itself the Revolutionary United Front (RUF) entered Sierra Leone from Liberia, launching a rebellion to overthrow the APC government. The outbreak of the war brought fresh instability to Sierra Leone's politics. In 1992, Momoh was overthrown in a military coup by Captain Valentine Strasser, whose National Provisional Ruling Council (NPRC) ruled until it was itself overthrown in 1996, by his deputy, Brigadier Julius Maada Bio. Later in 1996, multi-party elections were held and won by Ahmad Tejan Kabbah, head of the SLPP, who pledged to bring about an end to the war. Peace negotiations failed, and in May 1997 President Kabbah was himself overthrown in a coup led by army major Johnny Paul Koroma, heading the Armed Forces Revolutionary Council (AFRC), which then invited the RUF to join them in the new government. Regional intervention by west African troops reinstated President Kabbah as president in March 1998. Only in 1999 was a peace agreement signed, and only in 2002, following the deployment of a large UN peacekeeping force, was the conflict finally declared over. Elections held the same year returned President Kabbah's SLPP to office for a second term.

When the NPRC took power, they launched a process to reform the 1991 constitution, with the professed aim of addressing the corruption of APC rule. Ahmed Tejan Kabbah, Solomon Berewa and Banda Thomas (subsequently president, vice-president and minister of internal affairs, respectively) were all members of the National Advisory Council appointed to lead the review process. The draft new constitution, published in 1994, proposed removing citizenship discrimination based on race or ethnicity and granting citizenship by birth to any person born to parents who were ordinarily resident in Sierra Leone for a continuous period of fifteen years. It also provided equal rights to naturalize, due process protections for the revocation of citizenship (by naturalization only), and excluded naturalized citizens from only the very highest offices of state. These reforms were never implemented, as governments came and went and civil war racked the country during the 1990s. Nevertheless, despite the continued racial basis of the law, both the minister of justice and the deputy defence minister were of Lebanese ancestry in the government of

Lebanese Sierra Leoneans tell their stories

Abraham Bamin came to Sierra Leone in the 1800s as one of the first Lebanese settlers in the country. He naturalized in his new-found home on 23 April 1907. His son Elias, born in the country, was at the forefront in the country's struggle for independence from Britain, and was jailed for his efforts. Despite his contribution, he was deprived of Sierra Leonean citizenship by the post-independence amendments to the Citizenship Act.

Elias's own son, Tommy, also born in Sierra Leone over sixty years ago, still lives in Freetown. He has not been granted citizenship. He has never been to Lebanon, does not speak a word of Arabic and speaks flawless Krio, Sierra Leone's lingua franca. Three generations on, his grown-up children can also not become Sierra Leoneans otherwise than by naturalization. They use British passports, from the country their grandfather resisted, because they cannot obtain the Sierra Leonean documents he struggled for.

A Lebanese lawyer opines that the legal changes and political appointments are all just a fig leaf, emphasizing that 'there is still legal and official xenophobia against people of Lebanese ancestry ... and it will stay forever until governments become more sincere with themselves'. Moreover, although the 2006 Citizenship Amendment Act has removed the gender discrimination, another member of the Lebanese community argues that nothing has changed: 'It is the race clause that should be expunged from the law books.'

Others complain that extortion at the hands of law enforcement agencies is commonplace, simply because the Lebanese are perceived as non-citizens. 'If we refuse to bribe law enforcement officers, we will pay far more to settle the courts,' one businessman laments. His mother is a native of Sierra Leone, which under the amended citizenship law makes him a citizen by birth; but he says his skin colour still draws all sorts of prejudices against him by other citizens.[67]

In 2002, Lila, a second-generation Lebanese woman, who had become a naturalized citizen in 1990, applied for a new passport [under the requirement to acquire a machine-readable version]. Her application was denied because, after scrutiny, the Immigration Office found that she had naturalized 'illegally' when she was over the age limit of 21. She could not, however, have obtained naturalization before the age of 21, because she had to wait for her father to take the Oath [of allegiance]. To qualify for a new passport, she had to take the Oath herself, but the President at the time had suspended the process of naturalization. On the surface, Immigration Officers seemed concerned about implementing Immigration Laws, but underlying that façade was a hidden message: By showing that the law cannot be used to facilitate renewal of the passport, the bribe expected is higher than it would be if the law had applied. An Officer suggested that Lila change her birth certificate to make the nationality of one of her parents Sierra Leonean, i.e. of Negro African descent. This way, she could obtain citizenship based on the amended [law] that states that one of her parents should be Sierra Leonean at her birth. After bribing the staff, she then took her falsified birth certificate to immigration, bribed the Immigration Officer and received a new passport.[68]

President Ahmad Tejan Kabbah; President Ernest Koroma, who took office after new elections in 2007, appointed one minister of mixed Lebanese ancestry, born to a native Sierra Leonean mother. Lebanese money remained important for the funding of political parties.

With the restoration of a stable civilian government since 2002, there have been some steps towards repealing the discriminatory provisions. In October 2006, a law was adopted to amend the 1973

Citizenship Act to remove gender discrimination in citizenship by descent. But at least one parent or grandparent still has to be 'of negro African descent', even though it can now be the 'mother or grandmother' as well as the 'father or grandfather'.[69] Dual citizenship was also permitted for the first time. The strict requirements for naturalization of those not of 'negro African descent' by the new definition were, however, left unchanged.[70] In 2004, the 1969 Non-citizens (Trade and Business) Act was repealed, freeing up foreign-owned business, though not addressing the underlying question of who is a foreigner.[71] In 2001, the immigration department announced that, in an effort to combat corruption, all Sierra Leonean passports had to be replaced by new, machine-readable passports.[72] The Law Reform Commission has also put forward proposals for a more thoroughgoing reform of citizenship law: the draft of a new Citizenship Act presented to the government in 2007 would finally do away with the racial and gender provisions of the existing law. Yet the law had yet to be presented to parliament by the end of 2008.

The Banyarwanda of eastern Democratic Republic of Congo

Together with that of Côte d'Ivoire, the post-independence history of the current Democratic Republic of Congo (DRC) most clearly illustrates the negative consequences for peace and security of a focus on authenticity and blood descent in citizenship matters. Even today, Congo's *jus sanguinis* citizenship law renders hundreds of thousands of people who have never lived in any other country doubtful as to their rights and legal status; and this uncertainty has repeatedly been used as a justification or excuse for taking up arms.

Because those affected are almost exclusively of the same skin colour as those whose right to Congolese citizenship has not been disputed, the connections to the crises of citizenship in Zimbabwe, Sierra Leone or Uganda have not been widely noted; yet, just as in those countries, one of the most critical issues in DRC for the past five decades has been the legal status today of the descendants of those who migrated during the colonial era – with the added complication of managing the integration or peaceful repatriation of hundreds of thousands of refugees of those ethnic groups that have arrived since 1960 from neighbouring countries.

In particular, the disputed status of the Kinyarwanda-speaking populations of the provinces of North and South Kivu in eastern DRC has been at the heart of the conflicts that have afflicted the region with devastating consequences since the early 1990s.

The two Congo wars, from 1996 to 1997 and from 1998 to 2003, involved most of the neighbouring countries and some farther afield,[73] killed perhaps hundreds of thousands of people in direct violence, may have indirectly caused the deaths of more than five million, and displaced millions more – hundreds of thousands of them across international borders.[74] In all this conflict, the question of who belongs to Congo and when they arrived has been central, with different laws setting the 'date of origin' variously at 1885, 1908, 1950 and 1960. The argument over who is an indigenous (*autochtone*) Congolese has come to dominate the discourse over settlement of the various conflicts, linking comparatively local disputes over resources (especially land) to national and regional wars.

The DRC, with a population estimated, in the absence of any census for several decades, to be around sixty million,[75] comprises several hundred ethnic groups: it is one of the most diverse countries in Africa. In North and South Kivu, among the most troubled provinces over the past fifteen years, the majority ethnic groups are the 'indigenous' Nande (North Kivu), Bashi and Barega (South Kivu), with substantial minority populations made up of other 'indigenes', including pygmy groups, and many speakers of Kinyarwanda, the language of Rwanda. Known collectively as Banyarwanda, these rwandophones are mainly Hutu, with a minority Tutsi. It is their status which has been and remains most contested in the conflict. While Tutsi are traditionally regarded as pastoralists, and Hutu and the 'indigenous' groups have been cultivators, most groups have always raised cattle when they can. As in many parts of Africa, disputes over land ownership and use both among and between pastoralists and cultivators have often been the trigger for wider conflict.

The origins of the Banyarwanda in DRC are diverse and much argued over. Some Congolese maintain that there are in fact no indigenous Banyarwanda in Congo. Parts of the territory that is now DRC were, however, prior to colonization, subject to the Rwandan king and already occupied by rwandophone populations. Their inhabitants (the Banyabwisha) became de facto Congolese citizens in February 1885, with the recognition of the Belgian king Leopold II's 'private' Congo Free State by the Berlin conference. In 1908 the Congo Free State was taken over by the Belgian government and became a colony of the Belgian state. In a 1910 agreement between Germany, Belgium and Britain, new borders were established, ceding some parts of what had been Congo Free State territory to the German colony of Rwanda, and other portions to the British colony of Uganda. Following the First World War, the German colonies of Rwanda and Burundi (whose language and ethnic make-up are close to those of Rwanda) were handed over to Belgium by the League of Nations in 1922, and in 1925 Belgium annexed them under the name Rwanda-Urundi to the Belgian Congo. The Belgian colonial administration then established a policy of organized transplantation of tens of thousands of Banyarwanda, both Hutu and Tutsi, from the already densely populated and famine-prone Rwanda and Burundi to districts in what is now North Kivu in eastern Congo (especially Masisi). These *transplantés* formed a source of labour (often forced) for agricultural plantations and mines established by the colonial authorities. Many others migrated independently of this programme.

One subgroup of the Banyarwanda today in DRC are for the most part descendants of Tutsi pastoralists who migrated to the area around Mulenge in what is now the province of South Kivu from Rwanda, Burundi and Tanzania, mainly in the eighteenth and nineteenth centuries, but some of them perhaps earlier. From the mid-1970s, this group began to use the term 'Banyamulenge' (people of Mulenge) to describe themselves, as part of a conscious effort by their leaders to affirm a separate identity from other South Kivu ethnic groups in the battle to increase their influence in regional and national politics – and to distinguish themselves from other, more recently arrived, Banyarwanda. From the mid-1990s, the term Banyamulenge often came to be used to mean 'Congolese Tutsi' in general.

Since independence, the Kivu provinces[76] have also taken in other Banyarwanda economic migrants as well as refugees fleeing violence in Rwanda and Burundi. In 1959, thousands of Tutsi fled to Congo during the pre-independence Hutu uprising against the prior Belgian-supported Tutsi dominance in Rwanda; and more refugees arrived in further outbreaks of violence in the early 1960s and 1973 (from Rwanda), in 1972 and 1978 (from Burundi), and in the early 1990s (from both Rwanda and Burundi), before the major influx – of hundreds of thousands – following the Rwandan genocide of Tutsi by extremist Hutu that began in April 1994. All those fleeing Rwanda were Tutsi until July 1994, when Tutsi rebel forces advancing from Uganda overthrew the Hutu extremist Rwandan government and ended the genocide. The ethnicity of those crossing the border then changed, and Western television screens became filled with startling images of massed Hutu refugees flooding into DRC; provoking an immediate relief effort where the genocide itself had notably failed to receive the attention it deserved.

The first law that governed nationality in Congo was a decree of 27 December 1892, which gave Congolese nationality to 'every child born in Congo of Congolese parents'. From 1908, the date of the transformation of the Congo Free State into the Belgian Congo, Congolese nationality no longer existed and Congolese became Belgian subjects, though deprived of the civil and political rights accorded to the white residents of the colony.

The status of the Kinyarwanda-speaking populations of eastern Congo was already controversial during the lead-up to independence of what became the Republic of Congo in 1960. The 1960 'Brussels Round Table' that negotiated the terms of independence was held just months after the arrival of tens of thousands of Tutsi refugees from the pre-independence violence in Rwanda. The status of these refugees and the *transplantés* of previous decades was a critical issue in the competition for power as independence approached and each party sought to co-opt the newcomers to increase its ethnic power base. There was heavy resistance to any grant of citizenship to the rwandophone immigrants, whose arrival had changed the ethnic calculations among political players. Resolution No. 2 of the Round Table ultimately stated that only those who were citizens under existing law – effectively the 1892 decree on nationality – would be able to vote and stand for office in the 1960 elections. The *transplantés* and refugees would be permitted to vote but not to stand for office.

Article 6 of the 'Luluabourg' Constitution of 1964 – the first constitution of the new state and the first legal determination of nationality – declared to be 'Congolese as of 30 June 1960 all persons one of whose ancestors was or had been a member of a tribe or part of a tribe established in the Congo before 18 October 1908', the date on which the Belgian Congo was created. This position was confirmed in the nationality law of 18 September 1965. The Banyarwanda (and others) who had migrated to Congo after 1908 were thus not citizens of the new state; which left their status as citizens of any state uncertain, since there was no possibility for many of them of returning to their country of origin. Arguments that the presence of *some* rwandophones on Congolese territory before 1908 meant that all could claim citizenship were not accepted.

In the years after independence there were outbreaks of violence in eastern Congo and elsewhere, as the political structures and coherence of the fragile new state came under immediate stress. The southern provinces of Katanga and Kasai began secessionist struggles. A period of national instability and civil war followed, ended in 1965 by a United States-backed coup putting Joseph-Désiré Mobutu in power. During this period a rebellion led by Pierre Mulele, formerly a minister in the cabinet of murdered prime minister Patrice Lumumba, broke out in Kivu and Orientale provinces in 1964. The Mulelist rebels espoused a variant

> ### *An indigene comments on the Kanyarwanda war*
>
> In the 1960s we had the war that we called Kanyarwanda.
> It was a war that was in some sense caused by the govern-
> ment because it was often the administrators who alerted
> the people to be against the Rwandans, the immigrants.
> Because they also, they were numerous and every time they
> looked for power, they were always excluded from power;
> they themselves, when they started to try to enter and share
> power with the others, the others would say, 'No, you are
> Rwandans, you have no claim on anything here, no question,
> and if you don't immediately quit your lands we are going
> to massacre you.'[77]

of communist philosophy, though support for their cause from
the dominant Bashi ethnic groups in South Kivu was based on
personal and ethnic alliances rather than ideology; the Banyamulenge sided with the then-Congolese National Army to crush the
revolt. In North Kivu, meanwhile, politicians of the 'indigenous'
ethnic groups mobilized supporters by labelling as foreigners
even those Banyarwanda who could trace their ancestry to the
Congolese side of the colonial borders from before 1908. From
1963 to 1965, fighting known as the 'Kanyarwanda war' pitted the
North Kivu Banyarwanda (Tutsi and Hutu) against the indigenous
Nande, Hunde and Nyanga as each group agitated for autonomous provinces and districts where they would be in control. Not
insignificantly, the Kanyarwanda war centred on Masisi, the loca-
tion of the largest number of Banyarwanda *transplantés*.

A new constitution was adopted in 1967 which maintained
the nationality rules of the 1964 constitution (and 1974 and 1978
revisions did not affect these provisions). Under the influence of
Barthélémy Bisengimana, however, a Tutsi from North Kivu appointed by President Mobutu to be the director of the president's
office and thus a figure of great power in the government, laws
were adopted to favour the position of the Banyarwanda. First, a

Natives and settlers

decree law adopted in 1971 specifically addressed the situation of persons originating from Rwanda and Burundi, provided that, if they were established in Congo before 30 June 1960, they had Congolese nationality.[78] In 1972, a general nationality law promulgated soon after the change of the country's name to Zaire moved the date back ten years, provided that persons originating from Rwanda or Burundi who had taken up residence before 1 January 1950 acquired Zairean nationality as of independence in 1960.[79] These highly controversial laws thus aimed to give citizenship by origin to those Banyarwanda who had arrived in the country after 1908, though there was no constitutional amendment to that effect. At the same time, Bisengimana favoured his ethnic group in official appointments, while an equally controversial land law was adopted in 1973 and used to benefit Tutsi elites: most of the colonial-era plantations in the Kivus then ended up in Banyarwanda hands.[80] It was during this period that the question of the status of the Banyarwanda in general and Tutsi in particular was elevated from a regional preoccupation to an issue of general national concern.

Bisengimana fell from favour in 1977, and the nationality question immediately returned to the table. In 1981, a new code of nationality was adopted by the Zairean parliament which reversed the changes of the 1970s, created the most exclusionary rules yet implemented, and effectively denationalized a large segment of the Banyarwanda population. Law No. 2 of 29 June 1981 provided nationality only for 'any person one of whose ancestors was a member of one of those tribes established in the territory of the Republic of Zaire as defined by its frontiers of 1 August 1885', the date on which the borders of the Congo Free State were officially recognized. This law took the date at which an ethnic group could claim to be 'indigenous' back to its farthest yet. In implementation of the law, Decree No. 061 of 1982 also cancelled the certificates of nationality issued under the law of 1972, leaving these people stateless unless they applied for naturalization.

Although some of the Banyarwanda could trace the arrival of their ancestors to a date preceding 1885, proof was difficult to establish and in practice they were treated as denationalized: they were prevented from participating in local elections during the 1980s, and many were expelled.[81] At the same time, however, a Banyarwanda elite still held wealth and land amassed from official patronage during the 1970s, an economic dominance that continued to fuel resentment of their position.

During the early 1990s, the regime of Joseph-Désiré Mobutu weakened under international pressure and the termination of United States support for his government with the end of the cold war, and he was forced to agree to the creation of a 'sovereign national conference' to debate the future structures of government in what was still Zaire. The prospect of elections and new political arrangements encouraged ethnic mobilization to control political space, using the language of autochthony where it was useful, or simple political deal-making where it was not: alliances formed and re-formed in different locations according to local politics. A 1991 population census to identify and register citizens in advance of anticipated elections contributed to the raising of tensions, since the voting power of the Banyarwanda, if recognized as nationals, would have a significant effect on the electoral outcomes. Ultimately, Banyarwanda were largely excluded from the sovereign national conference itself, as President Mobutu decided that delegates should represent only provinces where they could be considered 'indigenous'; a stipulation that also affected other ethnic groups straddled between provinces within Zaire's borders. A sub-commission of the national conference adopted a report proposing four categories of Banyarwanda – *autochtones* (from before 1885), *transplantés* (refugees) and *clandestins* (undocumented immigrants) – with only the first entitled to citizenship.

As these debates were going on in Kinshasa, the politics of Rwanda and Burundi also impacted negatively on the situation in the east. The Uganda-based Rwandan Patriotic Front (RPF) began its military campaign to overthrow the Hutu-controlled and discriminatory Rwandan government in 1990, and also organized and recruited among the Congolese Tutsi. Meanwhile, the

Rwandan government similarly formed links with and supported Hutu groupings within Congo's eastern provinces. In October 1993, a Tutsi-led coup in Burundi accompanied by massacres sent thousands of Hutu refugees across the borders.

In March 1993, the already tense situation erupted into violence in North Kivu. Electoral arithmetic, coupled with tensions over land use, had generated a coalition of 'indigenous' groups (led by the largest, the Nande) and Tutsi against the Hutu, especially in Masisi, where Hutu are the majority. The 'Masisi war', in which the provincial authorities encouraged attacks on Hutu in the region, began a process of 'ethnic cleansing' that has continued to date, with previously mixed-ethnicity communities becoming exclusively Hutu, Nande, Hunde, Nyanga, Tutsi and so on. In some areas, the Tutsi fought as part of a general Banyarwanda group; in others Hutu attacked Tutsi; in yet others they were outside the local conflict. In the short term, the Masisi war caused political damage to the Nande, as Governor Kalumbo, a Nande, was removed from office in July 1993.

Hostilities had hardly begun to die down under efforts to negotiate peace, when, from April 1994, the Rwandan civil war and genocide spilled over into Zaire. Rwandan Hutu extremists murdered nearly one million Rwandan Tutsi and Hutu who opposed the policy, in a government-organized campaign of violence that was unleashed just as negotiations to end the increasingly powerful RPF rebellion had seemed to reach a conclusion. First Rwandan Tutsis, and then, following the military success in Rwanda of the Tutsi-dominated RPF, several hundred thousand Hutus, including both innocent civilians and perpetrators of the genocide, fled across the border. They were then held in refugee camps placed largely among Hutu communities, thus further blurring the distinction between Congolese and Rwandan Hutu and potentially drastically altering the ethnic calculus of regional politics.

Hutu militia continued their violence against Zairean Tutsi after crossing the border, and divisions between Zairean Tutsi and Hutu were stirred into active violence. In some cases, Hunde,

Nande and Nyanga militia joined with Hutu *interahamwe* militia from the Rwandan genocide to attack Tutsi Banyarwanda; elsewhere Hutu militia attacked the 'indigenous' groups. Zairean government forces either stood by or actively assisted the Hutu militia in this violence against Tutsi, including by providing weapons; but other official comments supported 'indigenous' groups in efforts to expel all Banyarwanda. Several tens of thousands of Tutsi moved from Congo to Rwanda during late 1994 and 1995.

On 28 April 1995, the transitional parliament adopted a 'resolution on nationality' describing all Banyarwanda as foreigners 'who have acquired Zairean nationality fraudulently'. The resolution included a list of people to be arrested and expelled, the cancellation of any sale or transfer of assets, the replacement of existing governors and commanders with new officials, and the banning of Tutsi from all administrative and other posts.[82]

In South Kivu, in September 1995, the district commissioner of Uvira ordered an inventory of all property and land owned by the Banyamulenge. Evictions of South Kivu Banyamulenge from their homes became common, as were deportations to Rwanda or Burundi, escalating during 1996. Ultimatums were issued for the Banyamulenge to leave the country, and slogans adopted supporting ethnic cleansing: '*Opération rendre les rwandais au Rwanda*'; '*Bukavu et Uvira villes propres*'.[83] In early September, 'indigenous' ethnic militia, supported by government soldiers, began attacking Banyamulenge villages, killing and raping, and forcing survivors to flee. On 8 October 1996 the deputy governor of South Kivu decreed that all Banyamulenge must relocate to temporary camps within a week. On 31 October 1996, the Haut Conseil de la République – Parlement de Transition announced the expulsion of Rwandan, Burundian and Ugandan nationals. Scores of Banyamulenge were arrested and reports of executions and disappearances were widespread. Violence against Tutsi escalated throughout the eastern regions and many more refugees fled over the borders; many had their Zairean identity cards confiscated by guards at the border and destroyed.

In response to these physical and rhetorical attacks on their presence in Congo, from around September 1996 the South Kivu Banyamulenge organized and armed themselves both to rebel against the central government and to defend themselves from the militia now operating in their territory. In mid-October four groups (including both Banyamulenge and other, indigenous, ethnic groups) came together in an alliance of convenience to form the Alliance des Forces Démocratiques pour la Libération du Congo-Zaïre (ADFL). This became the catalyst for a regional war in which the ADFL rebels, who came to be led by Laurent-Désiré Kabila, a former Lumumbist originally from Katanga, were backed by both Rwanda and Uganda, whose troops crossed the border into Zaire in late 1996, and later by Angola. The Rwandan government stated that it was seeking to eliminate the organized Hutu militia that still raided into Rwanda from the refugee camps in Zairean territory; though Congolese largely regarded this argument as simply an excuse for Rwandan violation of Congolese territorial sovereignty and extraction of Congolese resources. By late 1996 a large percentage of the Hutu refugees had been driven back into Rwanda; ADFL soldiers were responsible for extensive and systematic massacres in this process. The rebels eventually ousted President Mobutu from power in May 1997 and installed Kabila as president in Kinshasa; as well as instituting their own administration in much of the east. The country was renamed the Democratic Republic of Congo.

Kabila's support among the Banyamulenge was effectively ended in August 1998 when he decided to expel Rwandese and Ugandan contingents from his army. A new war involving the Banyamulenge broke out in the east, in which the rebel Rassemblement Congolais pour la Démocratie-Goma (RCD-Goma), with the active backing of Rwanda, stated that it championed the cause of the Banyamulenge and Congolese Tutsi more generally. Among the disputed objectives of the RCD-Goma during the war (and in the negotiations that ended it) was the establishment of the specific administrative territory of Minembwe, where Banyamulenge would be in the majority. Rwanda itself again sent troops across the border, again justifying its presence in

DRC as self-defence, as well as part of an effort to protect the Banyamulenge communities.[84] Kabila also armed both 'Mai-Mai' and Congolese Hutu militia in response to the Rwandan army's supply of weapons to RCD-Goma.

For the Tutsi Banyarwanda of eastern Congo, including the Banyamulenge, the consequence of these events was that, whatever the reality for each individual, they were presumed by the Zairean/Congolese government and many of its people to be supporters of the Rwandan invaders and of the armed groups that the Rwandans were backing. The fact that Banyarwanda refugees often fled to Rwanda or Burundi for safety seemed to confirm conspiracy theorists' views that their true loyalties were over the border. Illegal extraction of Congo's resources by foreign interests – whether Rwandan, Ugandan or from farther afield – increased the general resentment of 'non-indigenous' involvement in the region. Hate-speech leaflets multiplied, denouncing Banyarwanda invaders and their puppets, who allegedly sought a central African Tutsi (or Banyarwanda in general; the categories slip) domination.[85] In 1998, hate speech was particularly virulent: among other official statements, Foreign Minister Abdulaiye Yerodia Ndombasi publicly asserted that Tutsi were 'vermin' worthy of 'extermination', allegedly leading directly to the massacre of several hundred Tutsi.[86]

After the assassination of Laurent-Désiré Kabila in January 2001, his son Joseph took over power. Joseph Kabila quickly began steps to end the war, and peace meetings were held in Lusaka, Zambia, and Sun City, South Africa, culminating in a 'global and all-inclusive agreement on the transition in the DRC' signed on 17 December 2002. A transitional government was formed in 2003, and elections held in 2006. The transitional constitution negotiated at Sun City provided, as a critical element of the effort to find a permanent solution to the discrimination that had contributed to the recent wars, that 'The ethnic groups and nationalities whose representatives and territories made up what became the Congo at independence should enjoy equal rights and equal protection of the law as citizens.'[87]

Nevertheless, violence among Banyarwanda populations and the 'indigenous' groups continued in North and South Kivu provinces, and between the supposedly newly integrated armed forces (Forces Armées de la République Démocratique du Congo, FARDC) and dissidents who refused to accept the settlement and rejected the government's control over the eastern parts of DRC.[88] Among those who returned to the bush were two officers of the RCD-Goma, General Laurent Nkunda (a Tutsi from North Kivu) and Colonel Jules Mutebusi (a member of the Banyamulenge community). During 2004, thousands of settlers from Rwanda crossed the border into DRC with Rwandan military support, and cleared land for farming in the Virunga National Park, a UNESCO World Heritage Site. Though the Rwandan government alleged that the operation was defensive, reports suggested that influential Rwandan businessmen intended to reap financial benefit from the new agricultural land.[89]

In November 2004, a new nationality law was adopted, after heated debate in the transitional parliament, which returned the foundation date for nationality to 1960, as it had been in the decree of 1971. But this law still founds Congolese nationality on ethnicity, rather than on birth, residence or other objective criteria, giving nationality by origin to 'every person belonging to the ethnic groups and nationalities of which the individuals and territory formed what became Congo at independence'.[90] No further guidance is given on which ethnic groups are included in this description. (Moreover, the upper house of parliament, the Senate, did not approve this critical article; though under the transitional constitution the views of the lower house took precedence.)

Law no. 04/028 of 24 December 2004 on the electoral register, meanwhile, provided for those wishing to register to vote to produce five witnesses who had already been registered, and had been resident for at least five years in one constituency, to give evidence of the applicant's citizenship. Although this process did not define citizenship on an ethnic basis, de facto discrimination remained pervasive. Many still argue that because the Banyarwanda are not regarded as having a 'territory' within Congo, they are not included within the 2004 law; meanwhile, the failure of the Congolese state to recognize Banyarwanda 'customary' claims to land remains one of the principal complaints of the Banyarwanda themselves.

A referendum in December 2005 overwhelmingly approved a new constitution, which came into force in 2006. Article 10 again recognizes members of ethnic groups that were present in the territory of the state at the time of independence in 1960 as citizens by origin of the DRC.[91] The 2004 law still remains in effect, with the new constitution providing an intended final settlement of the question of which groups are to be considered indigenous. In theory, the great majority of Banyarwanda should be included within these groups, but the wording of the law leaves a dangerous level of ambiguity in its interpretation. The rights of naturalized citizens were also substantially improved in the same legal reforms, and exclusions of naturalized citizens from public office – which had been extremely broad – restricted to only the very highest posts. Excluded from naturalization are those who are guilty of economic crimes or have worked for the profit of a foreign state, common accusations against the Banyarwanda.

Dual nationality remains prohibited under the law, though in 2006 the newly elected National Assembly hastily adopted a resolution purporting to bring in a six-month moratorium on the enforcement of the provision, after it emerged that a large number of politically important (and non-Banyarwanda) members of the Assembly in fact held two passports. A special committee was appointed to propose a solution to the problem. Two years later, the moratorium appeared to be still in effect, and the committee had still not reported.

An end to discrimination in practice will be difficult to achieve. In the context of the continued weakness of the central Congolese state and the presence of massive natural resources in eastern Congo, the temptation to manipulate the ethnic and citizenship issues for political or economic gain is likely to remain irresistible to some. In May 2006, during the election campaign,

Abdoulaye Yerodia, by then one of Congo's four vice-presidents in the transitional government and a supporter of presidential candidate Joseph Kabila, once again verbally attacked Congolese Tutsi at a rally in Goma, saying they should leave the country. In August 2007, hundreds of people rioted and attacked UN staff in the town of Moba, Katanga Province, after rumours of the return to their homes of displaced Banyamulenge.

The 2006 election confirmed the political eclipse of the Tutsi-dominated RCD-Goma: from being one of the four political forces governing the country during the transition period, it was wiped out electorally and ended up having virtually no political significance at the national level. A short-lived effort to re-create a united Hutu–Tutsi rwandophone coalition had also failed. And the Banyamulenge demand for Minembwe to be a territory of its own for the elections was denied. Laurent Nkunda, a Rwandan-trained Congolese Tutsi who had been a commander for the RCD in North Kivu and one of those who had refused to disarm in 2004, then returned to arms as self-appointed protector of the political and economic interests of Congolese Tutsi, under the name Congrès National pour la Défense du Peuple (CNDP). Active hostilities resumed in late 2006 and 2007, between the CNDP and the new Congolese army; and with a second armed Hutu group, known as the Forces Démocratiques de Libération du Rwanda (FDLR).

At January 2008 peace talks in Goma, provincial capital of North Kivu, the status of the Congolese Tutsi and the return of Congolese Tutsi refugees from Rwanda remained among the most difficult issues to resolve: Tutsi representatives at the talks complained of continued daily discrimination against their community, including exclusion from public office;[92] while 'indigenous' groups made clear that they regarded them still as immigrants, without a real claim on the land, and possibly working on behalf of the Rwandan government. Later the same year, CNDP forces with Rwandan backing once again went on the offensive, killing thousands, displacing hundreds of thousands, and threatening to overwhelm the UN forces protecting Goma.

Côte d'Ivoire's war of conjunctions: the 'and' and the 'or'

Just as in the DRC, the instability and civil war that have devastated Côte d'Ivoire's once prosperous economy since 1999, displacing some 750,000 people and causing 3 million to require humanitarian assistance, have some of their deepest roots in conflicts over the definition of who is a 'real' citizen of the country. As one of those who took up arms stated: 'We needed a war because we needed our identity cards.'[93]

Also as in the DRC, colonial-era cross-border migration, and the failure to create an effective and widely accepted legal regime for the integration of these people and their descendants as Ivorian citizens, sowed the seeds of today's tensions. More recent migration – in Côte d'Ivoire largely for economic reasons rather than as refugees from war in neighbouring states – kept the tensions alive and ready for exploitation by unscrupulous politicians.

Ethnic groups whose ancestors came from the 'right' side of the colonially established borders of Côte d'Ivoire have come to be victimized by their presumed association with more recent immigrants from the other side of those same borders; especially from the countries to the north, Mali and Burkina Faso. Systems for recognition of nationality have in practice often failed to make the distinction between the two groups, and have not provided for effective naturalization and integration procedures for long-term migrants and their descendants. Once politicians chose to exploit the legal ambiguities in the context of electoral and economic competition, war was ultimately the result.

The targets of ethnic discrimination in Côte d'Ivoire are two-fold: both foreigners, that is non-citizens who are resident in Côte d'Ivoire; and members of various northern-based ethnic groups collectively known in Côte d'Ivoire as Dioula, which fall within the larger ethno-cultural group of the Malinké, themselves a subgroup of the Mandé. It is commonly believed that the Dioula were migrants mainly from Mali and Guinea-Conakry and, unlike the traditional ruling elites in Côte d'Ivoire, they are predominantly Muslim. The 1998 population census revealed that of the

81

approximately fifteen million inhabitants of the country just over a quarter were non-citizens, more than half of them of Burkinabé origin, and almost half born in the country; of the 11 million citizens, approximately 35 per cent were Dioula.[94] Côte d'Ivoire is one of the top twenty countries in the world for absolute numbers of international migrants making up its population.[95]

Historical explanations for the perception of the Dioula as foreigners can be traced back to the 1920s and 1930s and the promotion of population movements by the then colonial power, France. In 1933 France modified the borders between its territories of Côte d'Ivoire and Burkina Faso, then called Haute Volta (Upper Volta). The new territory of Haute Côte d'Ivoire brought together three-quarters of the territory of Haute Volta and the northern parts of Côte d'Ivoire, in order to facilitate the forced transplantation of agricultural workers from Haute Volta to plantations farther south. Forced labour was ended in 1946, and the Haute Côte territory was redivided between Côte d'Ivoire and Haute Volta in 1947, though the policy of encouraging migration continued. By independence in 1960 up to 700,000 people had migrated from farther north to the present-day area of Côte d'Ivoire.

The independence constitution of 1960 left the details of nationality law to be determined by legislation. In 1961, the nationality law then gave 'nationality of origin' to every person born in Côte d'Ivoire unless both of his or her parents were foreigners. Acknowledging prior migration to Côte d'Ivoire, however, the law did allow children under eighteen born in Côte d'Ivoire of foreign parents to acquire Ivorian nationality 'by declaration' through a judicial process if they had lived in Côte d'Ivoire for more than five years. As a transitional provision, those who had their permanent residence in Côte d'Ivoire before independence could also be naturalized as citizens without further requirements if they applied within one year.[96] In 1972, amendments to the Ivorian nationality law repealed the possibility of claiming nationality by declaration, which had in any event been used by few people. Foreign nationals of whatever origin could in theory still acquire Ivorian citizenship by naturalization in the normal way under the apparently generous requirement of a five-year residence period.[97]

Côte d'Ivoire's first president, Félix Houphouët-Boigny, kept a close hold on power, favouring his own south-central Baoulé ethnic group, a subgroup of the Akan. Nevertheless, in the context of a strong post-independence economic boom, he and his Parti Démocratique de la Côte d'Ivoire (PDCI) continued to encourage economic migration from neighbouring African states and adopted a generous attitude towards both the pre-independence and more recent migrants, without ever directly addressing the question of citizenship. Côte d'Ivoire also received refugees, especially in the west of the country from Liberia, though in much smaller numbers than DRC came to host from Rwanda and Burundi. In the interests of building electoral support in the north and centre of the country, as well as satisfying a need for labour, Houphouët-Boigny promoted both the migration-friendly policy that 'the land belongs to those who work it' (*la terre appartient à ceux qui la cultivent*), and the relatively liberal grant of identification documents and political rights. From 1980, the electoral law provided that non-Ivorians of African origin would be allowed to register and vote in national elections.[98] Tensions related to migration were already evident: as early as 1970, a Bété uprising in the south-western plantation country briefly declared an independent state, whose demands included departure of the migrants. The uprising was brutally suppressed. In the 1990 elections, the main opposition party, the Front Populaire Ivoirien (FPI) led by Laurent Gbagbo (a Bété from the south-west with close links to the French Socialist Party), mobilized around a campaign that accused the PDCI of favouring foreigners.

Houphouët-Boigny died in 1993, just at the time that large falls in the global price of cocoa and coffee, Côte d'Ivoire's principal exports, brought economic recession; and with it, in the classic way, popular resentment against immigrants. Long-standing but previously suppressed tensions came to the fore and were exploited for political purposes by Houphouët-Boigny's successor, Henri Konan Bédié, also a Baoulé.

83

President Bédié abandoned Houphouët-Boigny's unofficial policy of ethnic balance in political appointments and introduced a new political definition of the concept of *ivoirité* ('Ivorian-ness') that had previously been used to promote common cultural values. A group of PDCI intellectuals devised a manifesto promoting a highly restrictive interpretation of Ivorian citizenship, limiting it to those whose parents were both members of one of the 'autochthonous' ethnic groups of Côte d'Ivoire. This new interpretation effectively defined the Dioula as foreigners and denied their right to live and hold property outside their 'traditional' area. Dioula faced ever-increasing difficulties in obtaining the identity cards and certificates of nationality necessary to claim their other citizenship rights, especially the right to vote and to hold land. Those who could not prove their citizenship and had Dioula names could often only obtain receipts that indicated they had made an application to obtain identity documents, but never actually obtained the cards.

The emphasis on *ivoirité* was designed both to undercut the FPI's ethno-nationalist demands and to exclude Bédié's strongest opponent for the presidency, Alassane Dramane Ouattara, an ethnic Dioula Muslim from the north of Côte d'Ivoire. Ouattara had been prime minister under Houphouët-Boigny (1990–93) and left the government to join and become the leader of a new opposition party, the Rassemblement des Républicains (RDR), which drew heavily on support from the largely Muslim north. Bédié accused Ouattara of not being a native Ivorian citizen but rather from Burkina Faso. The fact that Ouattara had spent most of his professional life outside the country working for the World Bank and the International Monetary Fund, responsible for the application of austerity programmes in Côte d'Ivoire as elsewhere in Africa, did not help his case.

Under the independence constitution and the electoral law in effect until the death of Boigny, the holders of the highest national offices – president of the republic and president or vice-president of the National Assembly – had, simply, to be Ivorian citizens. Bédié's administration changed the electoral law in

December 1994 and August 1995 to forbid individuals from running for these offices unless both their father *and* mother were of 'Ivorian origin'. This requirement was aimed at Ouattara (whose mother was said to be from Burkina Faso, though the origin of his parents was never proved), and he did not stand for president in the 1995 elections, which were won by Bédié. The 1995 electoral law also restricted the right to vote to citizens alone, a reversion to the pre-1980 position that immediately greatly increased the importance of citizenship to long-term migrants. During 1999, the government instituted a judicial investigation into Ouattara's nationality certificate, and it was annulled by a court on 27 October 1999 on the grounds of irregularity in its issue. Protests and riots followed, for which several RDR politicians were convicted under laws allowing organizers of demonstrations to be held responsible for violence. In November 1999, an arrest warrant for Ouattara was issued while he was staying abroad, on the grounds of alleged use of forged documents to support his eligibility to run in the elections in October 2000.

Bédié's administration also introduced changes to the land law, in part under pressure from the World Bank, which favoured the introduction of a system of written evidence of title to land rather than the unregistered systems of tenure that had existed up to then. Since the colonial period, the dominant system in the south-west of the country, for example, had been the *tutorat*, in which 'indigenous' landholders ceded land to others in exchange for a range of cultural and economic obligations, including payment in labour and cash. The 1998 land law provides that only the state, public entities and Ivorian citizens (*personnes physiques ivoiriennes*) have full rights to own land in rural areas. Customary rights have to be confirmed by a certificate acquired within ten years after publication of the land law. Rights of land users not suitable for transfer into exclusive title have no status under the law.[99]

In the context of the increasingly xenophobic national mood, the legislation provided a further basis for attacks on northerners and foreign migrants farming in their own right or working on others' land in the south and west of the country. During September 1999, more than ten thousand people, mainly Burkinabé migrants and Dioula, were expelled from their land and villages in the south-west without any intervention to protect them by the police, administrative or political authorities. Similar incidents continued into 2000.

It was against this background that General Robert Guéï, Bédié's retired chief of army (a Yacouba from the far west of the country), led Côte d'Ivoire's first *coup d'état* on 24 December 1999. Initially, it seemed that the new regime would roll back some of the political exclusion of the previous five years. Guéï formed a broad-based administration which included ministers from leading opposition parties, including the RDR and the FPI. Guéï pledged to clean up corruption, rewrite the constitution, and hold fresh elections. These stated ambitions were, however, soon diverted.

In late July 2000, a flawed referendum was held to approve a new constitution which, among other things, inserted into the constitution itself the requirements of Bédié's electoral laws that candidates for the presidency must be 'Ivorian by origin', born to a father *and* a mother who are themselves both Ivorian by origin.[100] Although the phrasing *'ivoirien d'origine'* could be argued to be simply a paraphrase of the nationality code's reference to 'nationality of origin' as opposed to 'nationality by acquisition' (by marriage, naturalization, etc.), the provision effectively created a new constitutional concept of *ivoirité*. The nationality code states that an individual has Ivorian 'nationality of origin' if born to one parent who is a citizen; and it still did so after the 2000 constitution was adopted. Yet the anchoring of the right to run for elected office in a requirement to prove 'Ivorian-ness of origin' by both paternal and maternal lineage led to a popular acceptance that to be Ivorian required something deeper than birth in the territory of a citizen parent. Rather, it confirmed the idea of a pure ancestry connected to Ivorian soil 'from time immemorial'. Following the referendum, the government of General Guéï led an 'identification campaign' during which many Dioula (or those with Dioula fathers) found themselves designated foreigners, despite the constitutional bill of rights' prohibition of discrimination on grounds of origin, race, ethnic group, sex or religion.

With the new constitution in place, presidential and parliamentary elections were held in October and December 2000. On 6 October, the Supreme Court, which had been dissolved and reconstituted following the 24 December coup and was widely believed to have been hand picked by Guéï himself, disqualified fourteen of the nineteen presidential candidates, including Ouattara and Bédié. Nevertheless, the coup leaders did not obtain the 'right' result. After early results showed Laurent Gbagbo leading in the 22 October presidential polls, General Guéï dissolved the National Electoral Commission and proclaimed himself the winner. Massive popular protests were met with a violent response, but General Guéï ultimately fled the capital and Gbagbo declared himself president. Ouattara's RDR demanded fresh elections, leading to further fighting characterized by religious and ethnic divides, as security forces and civilians supporting President Gbagbo clashed with the mostly Muslim northerners who formed the core of support for the RDR. President Gbagbo imposed a curfew and state of emergency; among other abuses, around sixty RDR supporters were killed by security forces in the 'massacre of Youpougon' on 29 October. On 30 November 2000, the Supreme Court barred Ouattara from standing in the parliamentary elections scheduled for 10 December, again because of questions about his citizenship. Nevertheless, the parliamentary election went ahead, boycotted by the RDR. The FPI won a slight majority, with ninety-six seats, followed by the former ruling party, the PDCI, which won ninety-four seats.

In March 2001, local elections were held, which the RDR contested, winning more constituencies than any other party. President Gbagbo immediately instituted a new process of national identification, claiming that most of those on the electoral roll were not citizens and therefore not eligible to vote. By the time of departmental elections in July 2002, some 20 per cent of potential voters had not obtained their new registration

Killed because of a name

Human Rights Watch described how, during violence surrounding the disputed elections of late 2000, 'Scores of victims from Mali, Burkina Faso, and Guinea, or Dioula from northern Côte d'Ivoire, described being dragged out of their homes, pulled off buses, stopped randomly in the street, or chased by groups of gendarmes or police. Numerous witnesses described members of non-northern ethnic groups being allowed to proceed at checkpoints and freed from detention after verifying their place of origin.'

In one witness statement taken by Human Rights Watch, a fifty-two-year-old bus driver who was captured while on his way home from work was one of seven men, including several foreigners, gunned down in a field near the railway. He was shot through the stomach and pretended he was dead. Three died on the spot and the others who were wounded were taken away:

'At around 2:00 p.m. on Thursday [October 26], as I was on my way home, I was halted by some gendarmes. I saw they had been capturing other people who were gathered off to one side. I gave my ID card and driver's licence to one of them and heard him ask his boss, "Look, this is a bus station worker from the local station." Then his boss replied, "I don't care about the place he works, just look where he comes from." When they saw I had a Dioula name, the boss

cards; others attempting to register found themselves given a foreign resident's card in place of a national identity document. When individuals attempted to register in their place of residence, they faced demands that they return to their 'village of origin' to establish their identity, or produce local witnesses from their 'village of origin' to testify to their citizenship. The director of the *Opération Nationale d'Identification* publicly stated that 'whoever claims to be Ivorian must have a village. Whoever said, "He's one of those Burkinabés who wants to burn the country and give it to Alassane [Ouattara]. But today we're going to do the burning."

'After a few minutes the gendarmes, there were about fifteen of them, marched us across the railway line. Then they made us take off all our clothes and told us to lie down. Among us were at least three Malians; two brothers and an older man. The two brothers tried to explain that they'd just come on the bus from Daloa to visit their parents. They still had their luggage bags. But the gendarmes didn't have time for explanations. They beat us in that place for about two hours. They kept saying one of their bosses had been killed, and that some of their guns had been stolen. While they were beating us we could hear a lot of shooting going on. I saw them opening fire into people's homes. It was like a war going on.

'Then at around 4:00 they told us to lay face down and said, "It's your turn now – look up at the sky and then look down at the earth and say good bye because we're going to finish you off." The gendarmes were all around; there was no way to escape. While lying there I'd given myself to God. But all I wanted to do was ask them permission to go say goodbye to my children and my wife. I could hear the two Malian brothers softly reciting their prayers, "there is but one God", and then the shooting started.'[101]

has done everything to forget the name of his village or who is incapable of showing he belongs to a village is a person without bearings and is so dangerous that we must ask him where he comes from'.[102] Those unable to produce proper documentation faced heavy fines and security-force harassment; ethnic violence in the mixed neighbourhoods of Abidjan and elsewhere escalated in this atmosphere of official permission. Alassane Ouattara was, however, given a certificate of nationality in June 2002.

In August 2002, facing pressure from the European Union and other international actors, President Gbagbo announced a government of national reconciliation, with representation of the four principal political parties in his cabinet. An attempt to demobilize many of the soldiers who had been brought into the army by General Guéï led, however, to a rebellion by some of those affected. Calling themselves the Mouvement Patriotique de Côte d'Ivoire (MPCI), they launched an attempted *coup d'état* on 19 September 2002. Though they failed to topple the central government, the rebels took control of the northern Ivorian town of Korhogo and the central town of Bouaké, engaging in fierce fighting with government soldiers. A short-lived ceasefire from mid-October gave way to further fighting in which the mid-west cocoa capital of Daloa saw heavy combat. The south-west also burst into conflict between and among autochthonous and immigrant groups; many immigrants or northerners were driven out. MPCI leader Guillaume Soro emphasized the foundation of the war in citizenship rights: 'Give us our identity cards and we hand over our Kalashnikovs.'[103]

The French government swiftly intervened with military force, launching *Operation Licorne* in September 2002 to reinforce troops already based in Côte d'Ivoire. Though controversial, because seen as self-interested and (in the first instance) hostile to Gbagbo's government, the intervention eventually helped to establish an often misnamed 'zone of confidence' in the main areas of tension. The French were soon joined by west African soldiers mandated by the Economic Community of West African States (ECOWAS), and from early 2003, the joint forces were authorized to act to re-establish security by the United Nations Security Council. Active fighting gradually gave way to a de facto partition of the country into two separate zones, controlled by the government of Gbagbo in the largely Christian south (including the south-west, retaken by government forces), and by the rebel 'New Forces'[104] led by Soro in the Muslim north.

The French also instituted a succession of peace negotiations and agreements that attempted to find a permanent solution to the conflict, variously under the auspices of the French government, ECOWAS, the African Union and the United Nations. As of 2008, a UN peacekeeping force established in early 2004 was still in place, supported by French troops operating under their own command. Throughout these negotiations and in successive agreements, the question of citizenship as well as of land ownership has been central.

In January 2003, the Linas-Marcoussis agreement signed in France by all major political parties failed to end active hostilities in Côte d'Ivoire, but set the framework followed in subsequent talks (Accra I, II, III; Pretoria I, II). Among other provisions aiming at the formation of a new government with jurisdiction over all the territory of Côte d'Ivoire it established the principle of a general revision of citizenship law, including that the conditions for eligibility to senior public offices should be that candidates hold Ivorian citizenship and have a father *or* – not *and* – a mother who were Ivorian by origin. On that basis, and under pressure from South Africa's then president, Thabo Mbeki, who played a role in facilitating talks, President Gbagbo confirmed in April 2005 that all signatories of the Marcoussis agreement (which included Ouattara) would be able to run for office in the next presidential elections.[105]

Powerful economic interests affected by the war also intervened to ensure some changes to the 1998 land law in relation to the rights of non-citizens. Reforms adopted in August 2004 recognized the rights of those non-citizens who could prove legal title to land dating before the 1998 land law, including the right to pass title to others; though with the requirement that these rights took effect only if the owners were specifically listed in a decree of the Council of Ministers.[106] The new law did not change the situation of those who did not have written evidence of ownership and only just over one hundred non-citizens actually benefited from this legislation, out of which more than a third were French agribusinesses. The vast majority of non-citizen landholders were still left with no secure tenure.

Two laws adopted in late 2004 revised the nationality code and established temporary special naturalization procedures that partially addressed some of the nationality problems.[107] The revisions to the nationality code related to the acquisition of citizenship by marriage and provided explicit restrictions on the exercise of public office by naturalized citizens. The temporary special naturalization procedures applied to all those who had been allowed to claim nationality from 1961 either during the transitional period of one year or until the procedures were repealed by the amendments to the nationality code in 1972 (that is, those aged under twenty-one at the date of independence and born in Côte d'Ivoire of foreign parents, those born in Côte d'Ivoire of foreign parents between 1960 and 1973, and those who habitually lived in Côte d'Ivoire before independence). The law established that people in these categories could, during a limited period, apply for naturalization with written evidence in the form of an original birth certificate or a *jugement supplétif* from a court, a form of late certification of birth in the country.

The Council of Ministers finally adopted the decree providing for implementation of the law on special naturalization procedures on 31 May 2006,[108] starting an initial one-year period for those who wished to apply for naturalization under its provisions. The government then implemented a programme of identification through a process of hearings before mobile magistrates' courts (*audiences foraines*). The process aimed to provide those eligible with the *jugement supplétif* required under the special law, an essential prerequisite to obtain a national identification card or a certificate of nationality. Claiming citizenship is then a second step of the process, regulated by existing law; the *jugements supplétifs* do not in themselves confer any authoritative indication of citizenship.

This special identification process was repeatedly postponed by Gbagbo and interrupted by his supporters: in July/August 2006 the FPI's Jeunes Patriotes (Young Patriots) militia responded to a party leadership call to arms and brought the hearings to a halt by staging violent demonstrations and attacking foreigners and opposition party organizers.

While this process was still blocked, Gbagbo and Soro finally signed an agreement in March 2007 in Ouagadougou, creating a government of national reconciliation. Gbagbo was to be president and Soro prime minister. Further measures agreed for the reunification of the country included the redeployment of administrative authorities throughout the country, the demobilization of militias, the disarmament of former combatants, a process to provide identity cards for the population, and the organization of fresh democratic elections within one year. The identification process then resumed, and by mid-May 2008, when it was declared completed after time extensions, the *audiences foraines* had issued more than 600,000 *jugements supplétifs*.[109]

Despite the 'flame of peace ceremony' in Bouaké on 30 July 2007 which symbolized the end of the war and the beginning of the reconciliation process, the establishment of a lasting peace remained uncertain. Elections were repeatedly postponed, owing to problems and delays with the voter registration process, closely linked to the wider identification issues. Fundamental questions remained about how the government would ensure the participation of all eligible Ivorian citizens and the long-term rights of the Dioula community. Many theoretically eligible people had not benefited from the *audiences foraines*; and others who could in theory naturalize under the regular provisions of the nationality code are regarded as foreign in practice, and unable in particular to enjoy secure tenure of land. Côte d'Ivoire was far from resolving its citizenship problems.

Tiken Jah Fakoly, 'Où veux-tu que j'aille'

Où veux-tu que j'aille?
Pourquoi veux-tu que j'm'en
*   aille?*
Où veux-tu que j'aille?

T'as brûlé ma maison d'Abidjan
Parce-que je ne suis pas de ton
*   clan*
Mon grand-père t'a tout donné
Mon papa a tant sué
Moi je suis né là,
Pourquoi veux-tu que j'm'en
*   aille?*
Front la racaille!
Où veux-tu que j'aille?

Où veux-tu que j'aille?
Pourquoi veux-tu que j'm'en
*   aille?*
Où veux-tu que j'aille?
...

Nous sommes tous nés là
Exilés sans autre choix
Nos grands-pères se sont sacri-
*   fiés (tirailleurs!)*

Nos papas se sont intégrés
Même si on nous traite
*   d'étrangers*
Pourquoi veux-tu qu'on s'en
*   aille?*
Front la pagaille

Où veux-tu qu'on aille?
Mais où veux-tu que j'aille?
Pourquoi veux-tu qu'on s'en
*   aille?*
Où veux-tu qu'on aille?

Dans les années soixante
On a fait appeler là nos frères
Rappelés au bord de la mer!
Bukinabés, maliens et afri-
*   cains*
Pourquoi veux-tu qu'ils s'en
*   aillent, compatriotes?*
Pourquoi tu en as honte?

Où veux-tu qu'on aille?
Pourquoi veux-tu que j'm'en
*   aille?*
Où veux-tu qu'on aille?

Tiken Jah Fakoly, 'Where do you want me to go?'

Where do you want me to go?
Why do you want me to go?
Where do you want me to go?

You burnt my house in Abidjan
Because I am not from your
    clan
My grandfather gave you every-
    thing
My father sweated so much
    for you
Me, I was born there,
Why do you want me to go?
Rabble rousers!
Where do you want me to go?

Where do you want me to go?
Why do you want me to go?
Where do you want me to go?

...

We were all born there
Exiles without any choice
Our grandfathers were sacri-
    ficed (tirailleurs![110])
Our fathers were integrated

Even if we are treated as
    strangers
Why do you want us to go?
Coalition for chaos

Where do you want us to
    go?
But where do you want me
    to go?
Why do you want us to go?
Where do you want us to go?

In the 1960s
We called on our brothers
To come to the edge of the
    sea!
Burkinabés, Malians and
    Africans
Why do you want them to
    go, compatriots?
Why are you ashamed of
    them?

Where do you want us to go?
Why do you want me to go?
Where do you want us to go?

4 | Mass denationalization and expulsion

The African Charter on Human and Peoples' Rights, uniquely among similar international human rights treaties, includes a specific prohibition on 'mass expulsion of non-nationals', defined as 'that which is aimed at national, racial, ethnic or religious groups'. The drafters of the charter, which was adopted in 1981 and entered into force in 1986, had in mind the experience of several African countries during the 1960s and 1970s, in which governments had denationalized and expelled the descendants of immigrant groups. The best-known of these expulsions was perhaps that of the Ugandan Asians driven out of the country by the government of Idi Amin (see above, p. 50, on the situation of East African Asians).

Yet many other African countries have also expelled citizens or non-citizens en masse, often in appalling conditions, and without any right to a hearing to determine their right to remain. Uganda itself, in a much less well-known episode that took place under President Milton Obote, displaced a large number of Banyarwanda in the early 1980s, including some 40,000 people who claimed Ugandan citizenship and 31,000 people registered with the Office of the UN High Commissioner for Refugees (UNHCR), forcing most of them to seek refuge in Rwanda.[1] Nigeria expelled Ghanaians immediately after independence, and again in 1983 around 1.5 to 2 million foreigners, of which an estimated one million were Ghanaians. In 1965 and 1970 Ghana also expelled several hundred thousand foreigners, many of them Nigerian, including children born in the country.[2]

In the mid-1990s, an estimated half a million Chadian and other nationality workers were expelled from Nigeria, including among them many who had been legally established in the country for many years.[3] Gabon, which hosts many migrant workers in its oil industry, expelled foreigners on several occasions in the 1990s, and in September 1994 enacted laws that required foreigners to pay residence fees of up to $1,200 or leave the country by 15 February 1995: 55,000 foreign nationals left the country, and 15,000 legalized their residency; around a thousand were detained and held in a camp before being repatriated.[4] The African Commission on Human and Peoples' Rights ruled against Zambia for expelling several hundred West Africans in 1992; Angola for the expulsion of West Africans in 1996; and Guinea for massive violations against Sierra Leonean refugees, including expulsions, in 2000.[5] In 2004 and 2005, Angola's *Operación Brilhante* led to the deportation of more than a quarter of a million foreign citizens involved in artisanal diamond mining, mainly from the two Congos and West Africa.[6] In 2006, Niger began deportations of thousands of Mahamid Arabs who had fled insecurity in Chad during the 1980s.[7]

Libya, while repeatedly stating a policy of welcoming Arab and African immigrants, has expelled sub-Saharan and other North Africans in successive campaigns, with a particularly serious round of violence against foreigners in 2000.[8] It was thus not an accident that a meeting of African Union (AU) ministers on immigration gathered in Tripoli in June 2005 specifically called for a protocol to the African Charter on deportations and expulsions, to address the concerns of due process and respect for human rights.[9]

Yet the mass expulsions that are of most concern are not those that affect recent immigrants, but rather those targeted at populations that until the date that political events turned against them had always been regarded as citizens, with a complete right to stay in their country of origin and protection against any such action. Two especially egregious cases are described below: the reciprocal expulsion of people of Ethiopian or Eritrean origin from each other's territory in the late 1990s, and the expulsion of black Mauritanians from their country, starting in 1989 and lasting into the early 1990s.

Eritrea/Ethiopia: the fallout from an old-fashioned war

In 1998, former comrades-in-arms against dictatorship in Ethiopia's central government, who had together successfully overthrown that regime and then, to the world's admiration, peacefully managed the process of creating a new state of Eritrea along Ethiopia's northern border, decided to turn their guns on each other instead. The brutal war that followed between the Ethiopian and Eritrean armies, fought out in an arid mountainous version of First World War trenches, devastated the lives of tens of thousands: not only the soldiers who were killed and injured and their families; but of all those who became instant suspected traitors in the land of their birth. The conflict rendered people born of parents from the 'wrong' side of the border of what had been one country effectively stateless, unwelcome and persecuted.[10]

Though Ethiopia was never formally colonized, Eritrea was an Italian colony from the late nineteenth century until 1941, when British troops advancing from Sudan defeated the Italians during the Second World War. Following a period of British military administration, the United Nations adopted a resolution in 1950 designating Eritrea an autonomous unit federated to Ethiopia. In 1962, Ethiopian emperor Haile Selassie unilaterally annexed Eritrea and declared it a province of Ethiopia; residents of Eritrea without another nationality were declared to be Ethiopian nationals. The Eritrean People's Liberation Front (EPLF) began an armed struggle against Ethiopian rule; following the 1974 overthrow of the emperor by the brutal military government known as the Derg, they joined with the Tigrayan People's Liberation Front (TPLF) of northern Ethiopia and other ethnically based armed groups in the alliance known as the Ethiopian Peoples' Revolutionary Democratic Front (EPRDF).

In 1991, the EPRDF finally defeated the Derg, and the new Ethiopian transitional government immediately approved – as promised within the alliance – a referendum on the status of Eritrea. All individuals identifying themselves as Eritrean, including those living within the borders of what would become Ethiopia, were allowed to register and vote, provided they obtained an 'identification card' issued by the Eritrean provisional government. More than 1.1 million people registered; including more than 300,000 outside the country, 60,000 of whom were in Ethiopia. The referendum was held in 1993 under UN supervision; the vote was 99 per cent in favour of independence, and a new state was formed. The two governments agreed that 'until such time that the citizens of one of the sides residing in the other's territory are fully identified and until the issue of citizenship is settled in both countries, the traditional right of citizens of one side to live in the other's territory shall be respected'.[11]

In Eritrea, the Nationality Proclamation of 1992 provided that Eritrean nationals are those born of a father or mother 'of Eritrean origin' and defined 'Eritrean origin' to mean a person who was resident in Eritrea in 1933. Those who entered and resided in Eritrea between 1934 and 1951 are also entitled to a certificate of nationality on application. Any person who arrived in Eritrea in 1952 or later – including Ethiopians – must apply for naturalization like any other foreigner, showing a ten-year residence in Eritrea before 1974, or a twenty-year residence thereafter, and must renounce any other nationality. They must also not have 'committed anti-people acts during the liberation of the Eritrean people'.[12]

Ethiopia, meanwhile, adopted no new nationality law, though the 1995 constitution provided for Ethiopian citizenship for 'any woman or man either of whose parents is an Ethiopian citizen', and, while silent on dual citizenship, further stated that 'no Ethiopian citizen shall be deprived of his or her Ethiopian citizenship against his or her will'. The statute law in force, however, remained the Ethiopian Nationality Law of 1930, which stated that any Ethiopian citizen who acquired another nationality would lose his or her Ethiopian citizenship (as well as discriminating on the basis of gender in granting citizenship in general).[13] Nevertheless, as late as 1996, Ethiopia still affirmed that additional procedures were required for those who wished to substitute their Ethiopian with Eritrean nationality, in an agreement with Eritrea that Eritrean-Ethiopians should be made to choose between their two possible nationalities.[14]

Despite initial harmony between the governments of the two territories, there was popular resentment within Ethiopia at the perceived privileged status and economic dominance of Eritreans living in the country (as well as at the dominance of Tigrayans in the Ethiopian government). Tensions between the two governments began to develop also, especially on trade (newly landlocked Ethiopia relied heavily on access to the sea through Eritrea's Red Sea ports of Massawa and Assab) and on agreement of the border. In 1998, war erupted between them over the formal demarcation of the route of that border. Fighting continued over the following two years at varying levels of intensity, until repeated attempts to negotiate a truce eventually culminated in a comprehensive peace agreement in December 2000.

At the outbreak of the war, there were still around half a million people of Eritrean origin living in Ethiopia, including approximately 200,000 living in the Tigray border region. An estimated 100,000 Ethiopians were living in Eritrea.

In June 1998, approximately one month after the war began, Ethiopia issued a policy statement to the effect that the '550,000 Eritreans residing in Ethiopia' could continue to live and work in the country, although politically active individuals were ordered to leave the country and those in 'sensitive' jobs were told to take a mandatory leave of one month.[15] Despite this reassurance, the very next day saw the first wave of arrests and expulsions of prominent individuals of Eritrean origin, including those working for intergovernmental organizations based in Addis Ababa, and dismissals of those in government jobs. As the arrests and expulsions continued into 1999 and 2000, those affected were increasingly ordinary people with no particular status to attract the authorities' attention. Almost all those expelled from urban areas were detained in harsh conditions, often for weeks, before being transported in bus convoys on a journey of several days to the border. Rural people affected by the campaign were ordered to leave, and usually had to travel on foot, without their personal possessions. Ultimately, the Ethiopian authorities arrested, detained and deported some 75,000 people of Eritrean origin without any attempt at due process of law.

In July 1999, the Ethiopian authorities issued a press release stating that the Ethiopians of Eritrean origin who had registered to vote in the 1993 referendum on Eritrea's independence had thus assumed Eritrean citizenship; though that was clearly not the interpretation that any party put on the process at the time.[16] A month later all those who had registered for the referendum were required to register for alien residence permits with the Security, Immigration and Refugee Affairs Authority, to be renewed every six months. Business licences for these individuals were revoked, and assets frozen; despite procedures that were supposed to be in place to allow the appointment of others to oversee their property, many suffered huge losses.

The Eritrean government organized quickly to assist the expellees, registering them as refugees in the same way as other Eritrean exiles returning from abroad. Nevertheless, although the more economically and educationally advantaged integrated relatively quickly, many still reside in a UNHCR-administered camp in Eritrea and some still have no permanent identity papers.

During the first phase of the conflict, there was no official Eritrean policy of expulsion of Ethiopians, though Ethiopians were subject to popular abuse and official harassment, and many were in fact prevented from leaving by denial of the required exit visas. As the war continued, Eritrea's policy became more hostile. From August 1998 to January 1999, during a period of relative calm in the war, around 21,000 Ethiopians left Eritrea with the assistance of the International Committee of the Red Cross (ICRC). The Eritrean authorities claimed the departures were voluntary, though some intimidation was none the less reported by those concerned. In July 1999, Ethiopia asserted that some 41,000 of its citizens had been deported from Eritrea. A major Ethiopian offensive in May 2000 caused perhaps one-third of Eritrea's 3 million people to flee their homes. In early June 2000, Ethiopian citizens living in Asmara were told to

Expelled – never to return[17]

Ethiopian nurse B.H. was working for a humanitarian agency in Addis Ababa when war broke out between Ethiopia and Eritrea in May 1998. Then in her mid-fifties, she had lived in Ethiopia's capital all of her adult life. She traced her ancestry to Ethiopia's former province of Eritrea, which won its independence in 1993. She was widowed in 1989 from her Ethiopian husband – who had no Eritrean heritage – after more than twenty years of marriage. She had lived and raised her two children in Ethiopia.

In June 1998, Ethiopia authorities set in motion a campaign to round up, strip of all proof of Ethiopian citizenship, and deport Ethiopians of Eritrean origin from the country. Along with as many as 75,000 others, B.H. was taken into custody, denied her Ethiopian nationality, separated from her children, and deported to a purported homeland with which she had only distant ties. In Eritrea, parallel roundups of Ethiopian nationals ensued later in the course of the war. [...]

In September 1998 police sought out B.H. at her work in Addis Ababa and took her to the local police station for questioning by a 'processing committee'. As they asked her questions, the members of the committee took down information. B.H. noticed that an agent had marked down her nationality as 'Eritrean' – although he had never asked her to state her nationality:

'I asked him "what was that?"'

'He said "nationality."'

'"Why don't you ask me?" I told him.'

'He just laughed.'

B.H. said that during her entire ordeal she never doubted that the whole thing was a 'terrible mistake' on the part of the Ethiopian authorities. She believed that the expulsion bureaucracy would 'soon' discover its mistake and allow her to return to her family; indeed, she said that she patiently waited for that moment to arrive even as she was being transported to the border in a convoy of trucks and buses with 1,500 other deportees.

Five months after her expulsion, B.H. said it was still difficult for her to accept her rejection as an Ethiopian. What was most painful at the time of the interview, however, was her forced separation from her Ethiopian children.

Ethiopian nurse B.H. and tens of thousands of others were expelled en masse as enemy aliens, in groups of up to thousands at a time. Most were trucked or bussed to the border with Eritrea. Documents proving Ethiopian nationality were confiscated, property rights were cancelled, and travel papers in many instances were marked 'Expelled – Never to Return'. There was no opportunity for judicial review – or even for appeal of rulings through administrative processes. Thousands were detained for periods from a few days to a few months in difficult conditions; many were ill-treated at the time of their arrest or while in detention awaiting transit to Eritrea. Many endured great suffering while in detention and during gruelling journeys to the border.

register with the authorities 'in preparation for repatriation'. Soon after, the Eritrean government admitted holding 7,500 Ethiopian nationals in detention pending deportation, and started expelling batches of several hundred across the border. Property was also confiscated, affecting especially the large Ethiopian community in the port city of Assab. Figures collated by the ICRC and UN ultimately indicated that around seventy thousand people were expelled or repatriated from Eritrea to Ethiopia, just less than the mirroring figure, despite the Eritrean government continuing to deny it had any policy of expulsion. Individuals of Ethiopian descent still living in Eritrea who had not sought nationality by the time the war broke out in 1998 are considered aliens, dealt with according to the normal rules applicable to citizens of other countries living in Eritrea.

Those of Eritrean descent who were not expelled and remain in Ethiopia (an estimated 150,000) are not considered Ethiopians, but have not acquired another nationality. They are excluded from exercising citizenship rights, such as voting. They face lack of access to employment and education, and remain potentially subject to deportation. A 2002 law that bestowed special rights and privileges on 'foreign nationals of Ethiopian origin' singled out Eritreans who forfeited Ethiopian nationality and expressly excluded them from enjoying the new rights and privileges.[18] In late 2003 and early 2004 the situation improved as relations between Ethiopia and Eritrea also eased somewhat, with the publication of a new Proclamation on Ethiopian Nationality that made naturalization easier, and the adoption by the immigration authorities of an internal directive on the residence status of Eritrean nationals living in Ethiopia. But although many people of Eritrean origin living in Ethiopia were able to reacquire citizenship under this proclamation, problems are still reported in obtaining national identification cards, including delays of several years and interrogation by immigration officials. Moreover, the directive states that a residence permit may be cancelled 'where the bearer ... is found to be an undesirable foreigner'. An Ethiopian of Eritrean descent interviewed in early 2008 observed that 'the gap between law and implementation is like the space between the sun and the moon, and no one knows how to close it'.[19]

In 2004, the independent Claims Commission established under the December 2000 peace agreement adjudicated on the nationality of the citizens of Ethiopia and Eritrea after the splitting of the two countries in 1993. Ethiopia had tried to justify the denationalizations and forced population transfers during the war by arguing that those Ethiopians who registered as Eritreans for the referendum in 1993 had thereby lost their nationality. Eritrea argued that they could not have done so because there was no Eritrea in existence at that point. The Claims Commission found that, under the 'unusual transitional circumstances' pertaining to the creation of Eritrea, those who qualified to participate in the referendum in fact acquired dual nationality.[20] The outbreak of the war did not of itself suspend this dual nationality, and Ethiopia's action in denying the nationality of the dual nationals had been arbitrary and unlawful.

Mauritania: non-Arabs unwelcome

In one of Africa's most dramatic examples of discriminatory denationalization, from April 1989 and over the next year, around 75,000 black Mauritanians with recognized citizenship were expelled from their country by their own government. The campaign took place in the context of a programme of compulsory Arabization conducted by the country's Arabic-speaking elite: its targets were non-Arabic speakers – who also happened to farm Mauritania's most fertile land.

The territory that is now Mauritania has for hundreds of years been inhabited by three principal groups: people of mixed Berber-Arab ancestry (collectively often known as Beydanes, literally 'white men', or Moors); those of dark skin colour who speak Arabic (a group known as Haratines, descended from slaves to the Berber-Arabs); and dark-skinned people who belong to sub-Saharan African ethnic groups (mainly the Fula/Peul,[21] Wolof, Soninké and Bambara, herders and cultivators who mostly lived in the south of the country, along the Senegal river valley). During the colonial era, blacks who led a more settled life were able to take greater advantage of educational opportunities and thus dominated the administrative structure. This turned around at independence, and since then political power has been in the hands of the Beydanes. In the mid-1980s, the government led by Maaouya Ould Sid'Ahmed Taya (president from 1984 to 2005) inaugurated a policy of Arabization: Arabic replaced French as the official language and other measures were taken to identify the state as Arab. The government also favoured the purchase of land by Beydanes in the Senegal river valley. Mauritanians whose mother tongue was not Arabic protested against these measures and political tensions rose.

The expulsions of 1989/90 took place in the context of a dispute between Mauritanian herders and Senegalese cultivators over grazing rights in the Senegal river valley, which erupted into communal violence in the capitals of Dakar and Nouakchott and brought the countries close to war. Each country then agreed to repatriate the other's citizens as a precaution against further bloodshed. The Mauritanian government seized on the repatriation process as an opportunity to begin systematic expulsion of black Mauritanian citizens: ultimately 60,000–65,000 were expelled to Senegal and 10,000–15,000 to Mali, while a few others fled to Chad.[22]

While most of the expelled refugees were stock breeders and peasant farmers, the policy also targeted soldiers, civil servants and senior executives. Many expellees were black Mauritanian government employees suspected of opposing the Arabization policy. These events began a 'campaign of terror' in which the Mauritanian army occupied its side of the Senegal river valley: several hundred villages were entirely emptied of their largely Fula inhabitants before being renamed and taken over by Moors and Haratines. Those dispossessed were forced to relinquish their identity cards and then transported in trucks, with or without their families, with few or no possessions. Others who were not themselves physically expelled fled the country to escape massacres and political persecution which continued throughout 1989 and 1990. The Mauritanian government claimed at the time that those expelled were of Senegalese nationality.[23]

In 2000, the African Commission on Human and Peoples' Rights found that the expellees had been arbitrarily deprived of their nationality, were entitled to return to Mauritania, and should have their identity documents and property restored, as well as receiving compensation for other harm.[24] This decision, however, was never implemented by President Taya's government.

From 1994, after a détente with Senegal, the Mauritanian government invited the deportees to return, and approximately thirty thousand refugees did go back between 1994 and 1997.

Many returnees, however, later left again for exile because they could not get back their lost properties, regain their jobs, or obtain national identity cards to replace those destroyed during the deportation in 1989. By the mid-1990s, UNHCR claimed there were 25,000 de facto stateless persons who had not repatriated from Senegal and Mali, while other estimates were 45,000 to 60,000.[25] As of early 2007, some 24,000 Mauritanians remained in 'sites' in northern Senegal[26] and several thousand more in Mali in conditions of poverty and marginalization.[27]

In a rare good news story, there are prospects for the repatriation and restoration of citizenship to the deportees. After the Ould Taya government was overthrown in a *coup d'état* in 2005, a period of democratic transition began that resulted in the election of a new government in April 2007. Freshly elected President Sidi Mohamed Ould Cheikh Abdallahi announced that the government intended to repatriate, restore to citizenship and compensate the refugees.[28]

Concrete steps to bring about the planned return have been undertaken. The government sent a delegation to visit the refugee camps in Senegal; UNCHR carried out a census of refugee households in Senegal and issued a call for support for donor funds to finance the repatriations. A tripartite agreement between Senegal, Mauritania and UNHCR was signed in October 2007. Mauritania undertook to restore the citizenship rights of the refugees, return their properties and reinstate former civil servants. Senegal undertook to provide all documents needed for the resettlement of returnees, as well as to facilitate the integration of Mauritanians who opted to remain in Senegal. The first refugees returned, with UNHCR assistance, in January 2008. A majority were resettled on their original property, and after some weeks' delay those in the first wave received Mauritanian identity cards. The entire process of repatriation was expected to take eighteen months.[29] Mauritanian refugees in Mali were also expected to return to Mauritania, under the same UNHCR repatriation operations.

By the end of July 2008, more than 4,500 deportees had

returned voluntarily to Mauritania. But on 6 August the government was overthrown in a fresh military coup. Though the new government stated that it would continue the repatriation process, its future was thrown into doubt. Even in the best-case scenario, much work would be needed to address entrenched discrimination against non-Arabic speakers and resolve the potential conflicts between returnees and those who, after the deportations, took control of the deportees' land and assets.[30]

5 | Internal citizenship in a federal state

Two states in Africa have responded to the challenges of multi-ethnicity by adopting explicitly federal constitutions. Nigeria has had a federal structure since independence, though the federating units have rapidly multiplied, making the individual units paradoxically less powerful; Ethiopia has adopted a federal constitution more recently, as a response to the highly central-ized structure of both the Ethiopian kingdom and the military rule of the Derg that followed it. The Ethiopian constitution remarkably provides for any self-defined group to make a bid for self-determination to the point of independence. In both cases, the federating units are designed to a large extent around ethnicity, with borders aimed at uniting the most homogenous population achievable within that area; though in both countries homogeneity is not even close to being achieved in areas of great diversity, while the definition of what is a single ethnicity can shift according to the political circumstances.

While both federal systems have brought advantages in terms of decentralization and local ownership of government, both have also brought their own problems. As the case studies be-low indicate, the Nigerian system in particular has inadvertently created a population of millions who are not regarded as holding full rights in the area where they live. The Ethiopian effort to give full realization to minority rights has had similar results, including the displacement of large numbers of people from areas now 'owned' by another group when the new constitution came into effect. Much as the creation of government structures that aim to resonate with popular loyalties and understanding may have many advantages, the two case studies indicate the importance of careful design of the details in relation to the entitlements of all citizens of the country, wherever they may live. Internal rules of belonging can be as important to individual rights as citizenship at the national level; and this can be as true in states whose constitutions are formally unitary, as the experience of DRC, Kenya and others has shown.[1]

Nigeria

Nigeria demonstrates within its own borders a concentrated microcosm of many of the problems of citizenship and identity that exist across Africa. In particular, a legal and policy distinction between those who are 'indigenous' to an area and those who are 'settlers' has led to the creation of a massive population of Nigerians who are 'foreigners' in the area where they live, without any of the benefits enjoyed by the 'citizens' of that place – and all without crossing any international border. Though these distinctions were in part originally designed to protect smaller ethnic groups from domination by the larger, it is today often difficult to find justification for them, or even to distinguish in historical terms between those whose ancestors were allegedly 'originally' in a place and those who supposedly came later.

Nigeria was created by amalgamation in 1914 of three separate territories: the Colony of Lagos in the south-west; the Protectorate of Southern Nigeria (including the rest of the southern half of the country) and the Protectorate of Northern Nigeria. At independence Nigeria comprised three regions: Northern, Western and Eastern, each dominated by one major ethnic nationality, the Hausa-Fulani, Yoruba and Igbo, respectively.[2] Nigeria's four constitutions since independence[3] have all grappled with the problem of ensuring an appropriate balance of power between the three largest ethnic groups that dominated the three original regions, and the remaining several hundred ethnic groups believed to live in the country. The sub-national units have beeen repeatedly divided, and the three original regions have become thirty-six states today. In addition, the 1979 constitution, aiming at ending the instability, military interventions and civil war that had characterized the country since independence in 1960, introduced a new concept of 'federal character': the idea that government positions at national level should be shared equitably among those coming from the different units that made up Nigeria's federal system.[4] This provision is repeated in the 1999 constitution currently in force; and the idea of federal character is reflected in policies at state and local levels. Other provisions of the constitution specifically require a spread of appointments: for example, the president is required to 'appoint at least one minister from each state, who shall be an indigene of the state'.[5] Yet 'indigene' is never defined.[6] At the same time, the constitution guarantees freedom from discrimination or special privilege on the basis of membership of 'a particular community, ethnic group, place of origin, sex, religion, or political opinion' – with the exception of any law related to state appointments.[7]

The lack of an official definition of an 'indigene' has caused many problems. In practice, it has been interpreted to mean a person whose ancestors are claimed to have been the 'original' occupants of a particular state or other territory; an interpretation that has no basis in the constitution itself. That is, at an internal Nigerian level a *jus sanguinis* approach to citizenship is adopted, to the exclusion of any admixture of *jus soli* principles that would give rights to an individual on the basis of residence or other real connection to the state or local government area concerned.

Being labelled as a 'non-indigene' of a state has serious consequences. Many states refuse to employ non-indigenes in their civil services; non-indigenes are charged higher fees at state universities and are usually not eligible for academic scholarships; non-indigenes may have difficulty in accessing any number of other government services, including police protection in case of ethnic violence. A non-indigene may vote, but will find it very hard to run for office in the area where he or she is resident. Local governments and states throughout Nigeria issue 'certificates of indigeneity' serving as proof of an individual's rights as an indigene of that area; and often these are available only to those whose father is an indigene, and not to children of a 'mixed' marriage if only the mother is from that place.

Internal citizenship

With the creation of ever more numerous units of the federal system, Nigerians are indigenes of ever smaller units of territory; and with the constitutional changes that have created these units, millions have found themselves instantly transformed into 'foreigners' in the only place of residence they have ever known. An indeterminate but undoubtedly large number of Nigerians are now in the situation where they can claim indigeneity in no state of the federation, leaving them in practice excluded from the benefits of citizenship in the only country to which they have any possible claim to those rights. To make matters worse, increasing ethnic tensions between 'indigenes' and 'settlers' in many states, coupled with pressure on jobs and economic opportunities, have resulted in more stringent enforcement of the rules discriminating against non-indigenes in recent years.

A range of Nigerian civil society organizations, including the Citizens' Forum for Constitutional Reform, have lobbied for years for an end to the official and unofficial policies of discrimination in effect, including drafting specific constitutional amendments to ensure this result. In 2004, a group of Nigerian senators sponsored a Residency Rights Bill that would have prohibited discrimination against non-indigenes who had lived and paid taxes in their state of residence for at least five years (with an exception related only to 'traditional heritage'; presumably such matters as chieftaincy titles).[8] The bill was never adopted, and with new elections in 2007 would need to start its passage through the National Assembly from the start.

Ethiopia

When the Ethiopian Peoples' Revolutionary Democratic Front (EPRDF) came to power in 1991, following a long war of rebellion against the highly centralized military Derg regime that had taken power in 1974, it made it one of its priorities to give political influence to minority ethnic groups. One of the first acts of the new government was even to allow the creation of the new country of Eritrea; much as it came to retreat on many aspects of that commitment later on (see Chapter 3 above). The preamble of the

1994 constitution, adopted after Eritrea was already independent, states that 'the Nations, Nationalities and Peoples of Ethiopia' proclaim their commitment to respect peoples' fundamental freedoms and rights, as well as those of the individual. The country was divided into nine states, essentially on the basis of language and ethnicity, each with 'equal rights and powers', interacting within a federal structure; and any group within those states is given the right to mobilize to create a new state within the federation, or even to claim the right to secede.[9] Each state, irrespective of population or territorial size, is represented in the House of the Federation, one of the two chambers of the federal parliament, by at least one representative.

The new states were given wide-ranging political and administrative powers, including the power to 'determine their respective working languages'. So, for example, the largest of the nine states, Oromia State, uses its own Oromo language for educational and administrative functions. Other states have also adopted a similar policy to a varying degree. Although Amharic is the working language of the federal government, all state languages are to enjoy equal recognition and each state may determine its own working language.[10]

Although the Ethiopian federal structure has considerably empowered millions of previously neglected or oppressed ethnic groups, it has – as in Nigeria – created a class of people who are not regarded as having full rights in the region they live in, even though they are Ethiopian citizens. The adoption of the new constitution also led to the second massive wave of internal displacement in Ethiopia in recent history. The first displacement took place following the 1974 popular revolution, when a military regime took power and nationalized all land in the country and returned possession to the peasants. As a result of this measure, tens of thousands of former landlords, most of whom ethnically belonged to the northern half of the country, were dispossessed and expelled. They received no compensation for the property they had to leave behind. The second wave of displacement occurred at the end of 1990s with the introduction of ethnic-based federalism and the independence of Eritrea. In some parts of the country, individuals who did not belong to the dominant ethnic group in the region felt unwelcome and left, often leaving behind all their belongings. Many of the displaced took refuge in Addis Ababa and other major towns, adding to the huge army of urban unemployed.

6 | The importance of paperwork

In 2007, the BBC website ran a discussion forum asking African readers 'Is a passport your right?' Respondents from across the continent and in the diaspora responded, detailing the trials that they undergone to obtain this most critical of citizenship documents. Repeatedly, they described the bribes they had to pay, the discrimination they faced, and the difficulties of producing documentation that proved their right to nationality and to travel documentation.

In practice, individual Africans far more often face the practical impossibility of obtaining official documentation than an explicit legal denial of nationality. Yet something as simple as a failure to register a birth or an indefinite delay in obtaining a national identification card upon reaching adulthood – processes regarded as purely administrative – can have consequences just as damaging and permanent as if denationalization had been enacted in the law.

In principle, recognition of citizenship should start at the time of birth. Birth registration is usually fundamental to the realization of all other citizenship rights: lack of birth certificates can prevent citizens from registering to vote, putting their children in school or entering them for public exams, accessing healthcare, or obtaining identity cards, passports or other important documents. Yet, according to UNICEF, the UN Children's Fund, 55 per cent of African children under five have not been registered, with the situation much worse in rural areas; in some countries more than 90 per cent of children are not registered.[1]

Access to documentation that can prove place of birth and parentage (critical steps in proving a right to citizenship) is thus already difficult in many countries, without the additional complications of ethnic and political discrimination. Nevertheless,

> *Citizens report the challenges of getting a passport*
>
> *Kenya*: I am a Kenyan Somali. Getting my passport was not easy at all, I now treasure it because of the process. I can't say am proud of it. It is our right to get passports, but in Kenya the process is a nightmare, it has now been politicized because of the upcoming election. Muslims in Kenya have been allocated a separate desk at the Migration. They don't need to be treated special ... but equal, like any other Kenyan.
>
> *Sierra Leone*: I have a passport and very proud of it. Holding a Sierra Leonean passport is not easy, more so if you are poor or your surname belongs to the Fullah tribe, like me! It cost a lot of money (for the average Sierra Leonean), it sometimes cost up to 300,000 Leones [US$100] which include 'see to see' for the fast tracking of the process. I believe a better option to get is to decentralize the process as people are better known in their communities. Everybody should be treated equally always.
>
> *Liberia*: Getting passport in your country of birth should be

people born of parents who are commonly acknowledged as being 'from' a place will ultimately be able to show their membership of the citizen group, should they need to obtain the documentation to do so. Those who are not in this position may face extreme difficulties in showing simply that they exist and have a claim to nationality in their state of residence, though it may be the only country they have ever known. Refusal to register births or accept applications for documentation is often perpetrated by low-level local officials or bureaucrats, who have little knowledge of the law, receive next to no supervision from the central government and whose actions are completely non-transparent and very difficult to appeal.

In Swaziland, for example, non-ethnic Swazis experience

a right not privilege, but in Liberia here, getting passport is being tribalized when it comes to certain ethnic groups like the Mandingo – which is unconstitutional, unjustifiable and unacceptable.

Sudan: I have my Sudanese passport though getting it wasn't easy, one has to first acquire a nationality card and then apply for it, and by the way, my fellow poor countrymen and those who have no relatives and no access to the Southern Capital, Juba (in terms of transport fee and poor roads to make it to the capital) are unable to get as it is only here in Juba in the whole South where they are issued.

Eritrea: In Eritrea getting a passport is a roller coaster. There are times when they issue passports to everyone, that is apparently when the issuing authority needs money, then they screen people when they issue exit visas. Children above ten years of age and young men and women till the age of forty-five are not allowed to travel outside the country, but family members and associates of the ruling system have it easy. And yet, they travel abroad and claim asylum.[2]

lengthy processing delays when seeking passports and citizenship documents, owing in part to the prejudice that mixed-race and white persons are not considered legitimate citizens. At the same time, the government has since independence treated the thousands of ethnic Swazis living across the border in South Africa as indistinguishable from citizens and routinely grants them Swazi documentation.[3] In Madagascar, members of the 2-million-strong Muslim community find that a Muslim-sounding name alone can delay a citizenship application indefinitely.[4]

Among the groups particularly affected by difficulties in documentation and registration are those who have been displaced by conflict, whether or not they have crossed an international border. Following the end of the long-running civil war in Angola, both those who became refugees in neighbouring countries and those who were internally displaced returned home in large numbers. While those who became refugees in most cases received assistance and documentation from UNHCR that enabled them to prove Angolan citizenship, the internally displaced who had never left the country were often in a worse situation.[5] The children of those displaced across borders who marry in the country of refuge face similar problems. In 2005, UNHCR was engaged in finding legal solutions for children born in the Democratic Republic of Congo of mixed Angolan and Congolese parentage and denied registration as citizens, despite nationality legislation granting citizenship of the DRC to a child with only one Congolese parent.[6]

When it comes to travel documentation, the law often favours arbitrary action. The Commonwealth African countries often follow the historical British law position that regarded the grant of passports and other travel documentation as being within the 'crown prerogative', a privilege and not a right.

Exploiting these legal loopholes, one of the most common actions of repressive governments seeking to silence their critics is to stop them travelling abroad: either by denying them a passport to start off with, or by confiscating existing passports when they try to leave the country. During 2007, for example, governments in Chad, Djibouti, Eritrea, Sudan and Zimbabwe – and no doubt other countries – denied or confiscated passports from individual trade unionists, human rights activists, opposition politicians or minority religious groups.[7] But litigation in some countries and new laws in others have begun to push back the tide of absolute administrative discretion: recent court cases in Zambia, Nigeria and Kenya have all ruled that a citizen is entitled to a passport, even though this is not provided for in legislation.[8] And in Uganda, the 1999 citizenship law explicitly provides for a right to a passport.[9]

The situation in Kenya provides a one-country illustration of problems faced across the continent. The basic administrative processes for birth registration and the issuing of national identity cards are extremely slow and inefficient to start off with; and then different groups of Kenyans from pastoralist, historical migrant or border populations face exclusions that compound the problems faced by all those who cannot buy their way out of the tangle of required paperwork. In some cases, they are left effectively stateless.

Kenya: no identity card, no rights

In law and practice, a large percentage of Kenya's population is deprived of the rights that are core to the ability to participate fully in the economic, social and political life of the country. While their right to citizenship may be acknowledged in theory, they have immense difficulties in obtaining the passports, identity cards and other paperwork that would prove this citizenship.

The law in Kenya provides for compulsory registration of births and deaths, and a new Children's Act brought wide-ranging reforms in 2001, including providing for every child to have the right to a name and nationality. Nevertheless, in practice, only 40 per cent of Kenya's infants are registered; in 2007, the UN Committee on the Rights of the Child noted its concern at 'the restrictive measures around birth registration, the discrimination with regard to the registration of children born out of wedlock and of non-Kenyan fathers, as well as the lack of mechanisms and infrastructure to facilitate birth registrations'.[10] The Citizenship Act, the most critical law to ensure that a right to nationality is respected in practice, remains unreformed and discriminatory.

The Registration of Persons Act, in effect since 1947, also provides for a compulsory system of national identity cards for all adults. Even those Kenyans who have birth certificates face problems in gaining their national identity cards once they reach adulthood. Birth certificates contain a note explicitly stating that they do not have any effect in determining the individual's right to nationality. Members of some ethnic groups find that once they turn eighteen they face an onerous vetting process before they can obtain the identity document that is an essential passport to so many national goods.

Investigations and hearings held by the Kenya National Human Rights Commission and by a 2002 Constitutional Review Commission brought repeated complaints from marginalized ethnic groups of burdensome screening processes before they could get identity cards or passports, or exercise the right to vote.[11] Kenyan Somalis, Nubians and others faced demands for bribes or complete refusal to grant documentation; though some managed to obtain registration by paying for the privilege. Kenyan women who had married non-Kenyans found that their children could not obtain identity documents, even though children born in Kenya with one Kenyan parent should have an automatic right to citizenship.[12]

Those who do not have a national identity card are unable to vote or contest any political office, and often cannot register their children in school, gain access to university, or obtain healthcare or other supposedly public services. The laws regulating marriage require presentation of an identity card for registration of the union. The non-registered may even be unable to enter government buildings to make a complaint about their situation, if they cannot produce alternative proof of identity. In the private sector, they may not be able to open a bank account or obtain employment in the formal economy.

Most of those affected by this discrimination are ethnic groups with origins in border areas, or with pastoralist lifestyles, including the Masai, Teso, Borana and especially the Somalis. These groups are also subject to harsh security procedures. Special regulations are set out for the North-Eastern Province and contiguous districts, allowing for the control of movement of specified ethnic nationalities or into 'prohibited zones'.[13] In these areas, the security forces have power to enter, search and arrest on suspicion and without warrant.[14] Constitutional protections for freedom of movement do not apply to restrictions imposed for 'the protection or control of nomadic peoples', among other circumstances.[15] Although two of the most draconian laws passed using these constitutional exceptions were repealed in 1997, the 1966 Preservation of Public Security Act is still in force and allows for special public security measures to restrict free movement (into, out of or within Kenya).[16]

Kenya hosts tens of thousands of refugees from Somalia, as well as a large Kenyan Somali population. The security forces have a long history of harassment of Somalis, whether refugees or Kenyans, who are consistently suspected of support for pan-Somali unity and universal engagement in banditry. In the aftermath of independence a secessionist movement was suppressed with great brutality, and episodes of military abuses have recurred since then.[17]

In November 1989, a newly introduced 'screening' procedure compelled all Kenyans of Somali origin to report with identity documents to the Kenyan authorities, for the purpose of 'registration of all Kenyan Somali and to expel those found sympathetic with Somalia'.[18] Vetting committees handed out identity cards to those that satisfied them; and confiscated existing cards from those that did not. Kenyan Somalis living in other provinces were told to go back to their 'home' district to register, a requirement not imposed on members of other ethnic groups.

Most Kenyan Somalis live in North-Eastern Province, but among the subgroups suddenly denationalized in this way were the roughly 3,500 Galje'el Somalis living in Tana River District, Coast Province. The Galje'el Somalis claim that their ancestors came from Wajir in North-Eastern Province in the mid-1930s and settled along the Tana river, where they had until the 1980s been regarded as Kenyan citizens, though they still faced exclusion from public services, lacking government-provided schools, clinics or drinking-water points. During the 1989 screening process, they were branded non-Kenyans, their identity cards were confiscated, they were told to leave for Somalia and many of them were displaced from their land. Their national identity cards have never been returned to those from whom they were confiscated, though their entitlement to citizenship was officially confirmed.[19] In 1999, the Galje'el were evicted from their main settlement and forcibly relocated some distance away with access to few if any services.[20]

In April 2005, the minister for immigration, registration of persons and refugees stated that those non-citizens (not only Somalis) who did not possess the necessary registration documents would be considered as staying illegally in Kenya and would therefore be deported to their countries of origin. The original deadline for the registration of non-citizens in Kenya was fixed for the end of June, later extended to 15 August 2005. Using this law, security forces once again raided the Galje'el communities. The Galje'el have obtained interim orders in court against the provincial administration and the attorney-general to stop any attempts to evict, harass, displace or render the community homeless or stateless.[21] But this has not changed the position on the ground. A 2008 letter addressed to a member of the Galje'el community stated that an application for an identity card could not be processed 'because the holder was declared to be non-Kenyan by the ... Task Force of 1989'.[22] Hundreds of people remain non-citizens in the country of their birth and sole residence.

More recently, the global politics of the 'war on terror' have impacted on the Kenyan Arab minority living in the coastal areas, who, unlike the Somalis, have not historically faced discrimination or challenge to their right to citizenship. In early 2005, the minister for immigration announced on the radio that any late (i.e. longer than six months after birth) registration of births in the coastal areas would have to be vetted by the central government. The justification given was that many terrorists come to the coastal regions and acquire Kenyan birth certificates illegally, and then easily get other relevant national documents and pass themselves off as Kenyans. In practice, the policy has made it harder for coastal Muslims to obtain identity documents, and embitters a population already resenting a general atmosphere of suspicion against them.[23]

Perhaps least well known, yet one of the worst affected groups, are the Kenyan Nubians, who came to Kenya with the British empire and who are still not accepted as 'native' by the state authorities.[24] The Nubians were conscripted into the British army from what is now Sudan, at the time administered jointly by Britain and Egypt. They became known as the King's African Rifles, or as askaris (the Arabic/Swahili word for soldier or guard), during the British expeditions of colonization in East Africa and in both world wars. When they were demobilized in Kenya they were not given any meaningful compensation or benefits, although many were allocated small plots of land for farming. In 1933, an official report had already criticized the British government's treatment of its former soldiers:

> We consider that the government had a clear duty to these
> ex-Askaris either to repatriate them or to find accommodation
> for them. They were told they might make their homes in
> Kibera and in our judgment they ought not to be moved without
> receiving a suitable land elsewhere and compensation for distur-
> bances, and we believe that similar obligations exist in respect of
> their widows or sons who are already householders at Kibera.[25]

Yet neither citizenship nor repatriation to Sudan was offered by the British authorities, and at Kenya's independence in 1963 the askaris remained in Kibera, where they had been settled. Kibera is now an enormous slum in Nairobi, which the Kenyan government has insisted is government land; local politicians have arranged for numerous parts of it to be given to groups of their supporters while the police and courts have refused to entertain Nubian protests.[26] The Nubian community faces suspicion from other communities around them. Many are unemployed, poor and essentially landless, now that the plots they once farmed have been appropriated for housing by other groups.

The Nubians today number more than 100,000, and their members are now the third or fourth generation of their family born in Kenya, yet they face enormous difficulties in obtaining recognition of their status as Kenyans in the form of national identification cards or passports. The Kenyan census, which until 1989 collected information on ethnic identity, did not list 'Nubian' among the forty-odd different indigenous ethnic groups. Nubians found themselves classified as 'other Kenyan', 'other African' or 'other Arab'. Even today, Nubians are routinely subjected to security vetting when they apply for identification documents on reaching adulthood, a process that can take years or may only be completed on payment of a bribe. Individuals can be called upon to produce their parents' or grandparents' identification documents to verify their origin, or asked irrelevant questions about acquaintances and family. Lack of documentation exposes Nubians to frequent arrest by police and ensures that the community is one of the poorest in Kenya.

In 2003, representatives of the Nubian community brought a case to the Kenyan courts seeking confirmation of their citizenship and the right to be issued with relevant official documents.[27] The Kenyan government argued that the case should be struck out on the grounds that it should have been brought against the British, that in any case it has been brought too late, and that the Nubians were not citizens. After more than three years of blocked progress at national level on procedural grounds, the Nubians took their case to the African Commission on Human and Peoples' Rights, requesting the premier continental human rights body to find in their favour in relation to numerous violations of the African Charter on Human and Peoples' Rights.[28] Since submission in 2005, this case has also been bogged down in procedural issues at the Commission.

The daily struggles of Nubians in Nairobi

Jaffar Hassan was born in 1979 in Kibera. She and her husband have four children and share a small home together with her brother. Jaffar's life story echoes the stories of thousands of other Nubians deprived of basic necessities. Whereas she says without hesitation that she is a citizen of Kenya, she has no means of proving that. 'My father, who died when I was very young, told me that I am,' she says. 'Nubians have a real problem getting any kind of identification documents.

If you have a Muslim name it is very difficult to do anything.' Jaffar explains that few Nubians can afford to pay the bribes that officials demand for birth certificates, and without connections in the government it is very difficult for Nubians to get identity cards and essentially impossible to get passports. 'Unlike other people here, Nubians have to go through a vetting process to get identity documents. If I wanted a passport for myself, they will ask for my parents' and grandparents' – sometimes even my great-grandfather's – birth certificates. My friend who is Kikuyu got a passport simply by showing her ID,' she says. 'I consider myself a Kenyan. I was born here and I don't have anywhere else to go even though people tell us "go home where you came from" all the time.'

Abdalla Ali Ramadhan was born in Mlimani in Eldama Ravine in 1955. He tried to get an ID card for many years, and finally succeeded in 1992. In 2004, he lost his ID card and tried to get a replacement. He was told, however, that he had to produce his deceased parents' and grandparents' birth certificates to get a new one – a requirement he was unable to meet. As a result, Abdalla has virtually no access to official transactions such as opening a bank account or voting. He also cannot be formally employed without an ID card, something which significantly contributes to unemployment and poverty among Nubians. Moreover, the risk of becoming a victim of police violence is significantly larger for people without identity documents as the police frequently demand to be shown national IDs to forestall arrest – something which Abdalla has experienced on several occasions.

Azizi Juma has a daughter who is three years old. Since autumn 2005 he has tried to get her a birth certificate and explains the bureaucratic process: 'I went to Sheria House where I was given a form to fill. I filled out the form and took it back. I was told to go to City Hall. At City Hall I was asked for my wife and daughter's clinic cards. I brought these cards back but I was told that they were not stamped. I had to return to the hospital and get them stamped. I took the stamped cards back to City Hall but could not find the person I was dealing with. After many visits, I found the officer and he told me to fill in a form B3. The form asked the names of the child, the father, and the mother and the date of birth of the child. I filled out the form. I then had to take the form to the Chief and Sub-Chief for signatures. I returned the form to the City Hall on Tuesday, 4 February 2006. I am still waiting for a response. I do not feel good about this process. The reason they are giving me all these hurdles is that I have a Nubian name.'[29]

7 | Excluding candidates and silencing critics

In 1999, the High Court in Zambia declared that Kenneth Kaunda, president of the country from 1964 to 1991, was not a citizen of the state he had governed for twenty-seven years. This surreal decision was the culmination of a process of manipulation of citizenship law blatantly aimed precisely at excluding the country's elder statesman from holding office once again. The same year, the courts in Côte d'Ivoire annulled the nationality certificate of former prime minister Alassane Ouattara, on the grounds that it had been irregularly issued (for the case of Alassane Outtara, see above, p. 81). These are just the two most high-profile cases in which governments have used and abused the laws and policies governing the grant of citizenship during the transition to independence of African states to attempt to secure their own hold on power.

Under international law, citizenship cannot be revoked against the person's will except in very restrictive circumstances, and in accordance with due process of law. Well-established principles forbid racial, ethnic or other discrimination in the grant or removal of citizenship, as well as the deprivation of citizenship if a person would then be stateless; and require that a system of challenge to such decisions should be available through the regular courts. A person cannot be expelled from his or her country of citizenship, no matter what the destination. Moreover, though a state may expel non-nationals from its territory or deport them to their alleged state of origin, this is allowed only if the action respects minimum rules of due process, including the right to challenge on an individual basis both the reasons for expulsion or deportation and the allegation that a person is in fact a foreigner. The African Commission on Human and Peoples' Rights – the guardian of the African Charter on Human and Peoples' Rights – has confirmed many of these rules at African level.

Revocation (or denial) of citizenship by naturalization can in some cases be unproblematic, most obviously if it has been obtained by fraud (though even then, an individual who would become stateless could make a strong case that it should not be allowed); most African citizenship laws include rules to this effect. It is also relatively uncontroversial for a naturalized citizen to be deprived of his or her nationality if the individual has committed a serious crime against the state, or fought for a foreign country against the state that has granted him or her its passport. Again, a wide range of African states make similar provisions. More problematic is the common provision that a person – in some cases whether naturalized or a citizen from birth – loses his or her nationality if he or she acquires the nationality of another state: the prohibition on dual citizenship. And some African states even allow for deprivation of citizenship by birth on virtually unlimited discretionary grounds, including vague allegations of disloyalty to the state. Whatever the legal grounds asserted, such provisions can always allow serious abuse when citizenship can – as is all too common – be taken away without any effective due process, on the discretion of a single official, and without any appeal to a court or other tribunal.

The Egyptian nationality law, for example, gives extensive powers to the executive to revoke citizenship, however obtained, including on the grounds that an individual has acquired another citizenship without the permission of the minister of the interior; enrolled in the military of another country or worked against the interests of the Egyptian state in various ways; and most contentiously if 'he was described as being a Zionist at any time' – allowing for deprivation of citizenship on simple denunciation by a fellow citizen. The law provides additional reasons for the revocation of citizenship from those who obtained it by naturalization. The Libyan nationality law repeats the provision on Zionism, and adds a power to revoke citizenship if a person has converted from Islam to another religion.

Examples of better-drafted law do exist. South Africa specifically provides that no citizen may be deprived of citizenship against his or her will; some other countries, such as Ghana, allow deprivation of citizenship (by naturalization only) on appropriately limited grounds, requiring reasons to be given and providing the right to challenge the decision in court.

Yet, as the cases below show, the right to a legal challenge is not always sufficient: the courts may not always rule in ways respectful of human rights principles, if the law is itself in violation of those principles.

Zambia: Kenneth Kaunda and others become instant foreigners

After twenty-seven years of one-party rule following independence, Zambia held multiparty presidential and parliamentary elections on 31 October 1991. The elections were won by the Movement for Multiparty Democracy (MMD), led by Frederick Chiluba. It was one of the first post-cold-war transitions on the African continent, much heralded as a model for other countries. Unfortunately, the initial promise of the transition was betrayed.

In 1993, the MMD fulfilled a campaign pledge to review the constitution by appointing a twenty-four-member review commission to collect views from the general public and provide proposals for the content of a new constitution. The Mwanakatwe Commission, named for its chairman John Mwanakatwe, released its report in June 1995, including a contentious recommendation for a constitutional amendment to require that both parents of any presidential candidate should be Zambians by birth. This clause would effectively disqualify former president Kenneth Kaunda, whose parents were Malawian missionaries, from standing for the presidency in the 1996 elections on the ticket of the United National Independence Party (UNIP) – the party that he had led during the independence struggle and which had been in power since 1964 until defeated by the MMD. The ruling party pushed the amendment through parliament in 1996, rather than providing for the recommendations to be agreed by a constituent assembly and subject to a referendum, as the Mwanakatwe Commission had recommended.[1]

The opposition Zambia Democratic Congress party unsuccessfully sought to prevent the adoption of the constitutional amendment through the courts.[2] Kaunda was thus not allowed to contest the 1996 elections, which were held in an atmosphere of severe threat to all opposition candidates;[3] in 1997 Kaunda was detained for several months during a general crackdown following an alleged coup attempt.

Chiluba's government had already began to use citizenship and immigration law to disable its political opponents. William Steven Banda and John Lyson Chinula – both leading members of UNIP – were separately deported to Malawi in 1994 under the Immigration and Deportation Act, on the grounds that they were not citizens and were 'likely to be a danger to peace and good order in Zambia'. Banda fought his deportation order in the courts, arguing that he had a Zambian National Registration Card and a passport and had used these freely for many years without challenge, but the Supreme Court ultimately denied his claim and he was forcibly deported. Chinula was given no opportunity to contest his deportation order before the courts at all and was immediately deported. The Malawian courts, however, declared both deportees not to be Malawian citizens.

Amnesty International complained to the African Commission on Human and Peoples' Rights on behalf of Banda and Chinula. In 1999, the Commission found that the deportations were politically motivated and that Zambia was in contravention of the African Charter by not applying due process in the two cases.[4] Chinula died in Malawi before the Commission concluded its consideration of the case; despite the ruling, the Zambian government did not allow William Banda to return until fresh elections brought the new government of President Levy Mwanawasa, still heading the MMD, in 2002.

In an ironic twist, following the 1996 elections, the dual-parentage clause was invoked to challenge in court the re-election of President Fredrick Chiluba. The petitioners alleged that Chiluba's father was not Zambian by birth and therefore Chiluba did not qualify to be elected president of Zambia. This time, the Supreme Court affirmed that citizenship must not be defined in discriminatory terms and questioned the rationale of the provision in the constitution requiring both parents of a presidential candidate to be Zambians by birth. The court held that, while the language of the amendment did not in fact exclude 'non-indigenous' Zambians from the presidency, if it had it might have violated the non-discrimination provisions elsewhere in the constitution. In any event, whichever of several proposed biographies was adopted, Chiluba's ancestors came from Northern Rhodesia (what is today Zambia) and his citizenship and eligibility for the presidency could not be questioned.[5]

In a subsequent case heard in 1999, petitioners from the MMD requested the court once again to review Kaunda's citizenship.[6] It was argued that the Zambian citizenship of Kaunda should be quashed, that Kaunda had never qualified to be elected president of Zambia, and that he should be declared to have ruled Zambia as president illegally. The High Court observed that Kaunda's own affidavit showed that he had renounced entitlement to Malawian citizenship on 21 June 1970. Thus, the High Court concluded that Kaunda had become a citizen of Malawi by descent when Malawi became independent (on 7 July 1964), but that at the time of the case he was neither a Zambian nor a Malawian citizen and thus a stateless person. Kaunda appealed to the Supreme Court, but the case was settled in 2000 and Kaunda's citizenship restored.

In 2001, the MMD split, after President Chiluba unsuccessfully sought a third term in office. Vice-President Christon Tembo formed a new party, the Forum for Democracy and Development (FDD). The government questioned the citizenship of both Tembo and Dipak Patel, another member of parliament who joined the FDD, who it alleged had not been a citizen when he first stood for election in 1991. Ironically, the MMD had refused citizenship to Majid Ticklay, a resident of Zambia since childhood but of Indian origin, to protect Tembo's own parliamentary seat when Ticklay wished to run for office in 1996.

In April 2003, President Mwanawasa appointed a fourth constitutional review commission, headed by lawyer Wila Mung'omba; and in August of the same year, a twenty-six-member Electoral Reform Technical Committee (ERTC) to analyse and make recommendations regarding the legal framework of the electoral process. The eligibility criteria to run for president were relevant to both processes. The Mung'omba Commission completed its work and mandate in December 2005. Most of the petitioners who addressed the subject of the parentage clause in the qualifications for presidential candidates argued for the provision be repealed. The Commission supported this view, on the basis also that the Supreme Court had doubted the constitutional validity of the parentage clause, and recommended that the requirement should be simply for the president to be a citizen 'by birth or descent' and not a dual citizen.[7] Responding to the ERTC report, which made the same recommendation, the Zambian government indicated that it also supported the repeal of the provision on parentage.[8] In 2007, President Mwanawasa established yet another constitution-drafting process under a National Constitutional Conference; following elections after Mwanawasa's untimely death in 2008, new president Rupiah Banda, also of the MMD, was expected to continue with the NCC process.

Botswana: the case of John Modise

John Modise was born in South Africa of Batswana parents, prior to the independence of Botswana, and brought up in Botswana. Until 1978, the year that he became a founder and leader of an opposition political party, Modise held Botswana citizenship without problems. In that year, the government of Botswana decided that Modise could not claim to have citizenship by descent,[9] and the Office of the President declared Modise a prohibited immigrant. His arrest and deportation to South Africa followed soon thereafter. Even one of Africa's most stable democracies resorted to underhand means to prevent challenge to the status quo.

Modise was not given the chance to challenge the deportation in court and his removal prevented him from following up on an application for a temporary work permit which, if granted, would have allowed him to remain in Botswana. Four days after the first deportation, Modise re-entered Botswana and was arrested, charged with illegally entering the country as a prohibited immigrant, and deported again without a hearing. After his third attempt to enter Botswana he was again arrested and charged with the same crime, but was this time sentenced to a ten-month prison term. Modise filed an appeal but before it was heard he was again deported to South Africa.

The South African government did not recognize Modise as a citizen either and he was forced to settle in the then 'homeland' of Bophuthatswana, where he lived for seven years before he was again deported, this time to the no-man's-land border zone between Botswana and South Africa, where he lived for several months. Modise was finally allowed to re-enter Botswana on humanitarian grounds, but was forced to remain on the basis of temporary residence permits, which were renewed every three months at the discretion of the Ministry of Home Affairs.[10]

The effect on Modise of being rendered stateless, declared a prohibited immigrant, deported numerous times and kept in a prolonged state of insecurity was to bankrupt him, disrupt his personal life and effectively quash his political aspirations. In 1993, a complaint was filed on his behalf with the African Commission on Human and Peoples' Rights, which was finally decided in 2000 after many attempts to reach an amicable resolution. The Botswana government attempted a solution to the problem for many years by offering Modise citizenship by naturalization: but though citizenship by naturalization extends nearly all of the same rights as are conferred on those categorized citizens by birth or descent under the law, the constitution places limits with regard to the holding of political office. As a naturalized citizen Modise would not be eligible to hold the highest political office in Botswana – that of president. Citizenship by naturalization would also not guarantee citizenship of his children, unless it was granted retroactively.

The African Commission ruled in favour of Modise, found

Botswana to be in violation of Articles 5 and 7 of the African Charter on Human and Peoples' Rights and recommended that Botswana recognize Modise's citizenship by descent. The African Commission held that

> while [restrictions on holding public office] may not seriously affect most individuals, it is apparent that for Mr Modise such is a legal disability of grave consequence. Considering the fact that his first deportation [and declaration as a prohibited immigrant] came soon after he founded an opposition political party, it suggests a pattern of action designed to hamper his political participation. When taken together with the above action, granting the Complainant citizenship by [naturalization] has, therefore, gravely deprived him of one of his most cherished fundamental rights, to freely participate in the government of his country, either directly or through elected representatives.[11]

The Botswana government has, however, never backed down from its initial objections to Modise's claim to citizenship and the case finally ended with Modise being forced to accept Botswana citizenship by naturalization.[12]

Swaziland: critics are 'un-Swazi'

Since Swaziland gained independence from the United Kingdom in 1968, its rulers have chosen to emphasize an exclusive ethnic identity for the country. Tradition has been invoked to uphold a monarchical system that has never subjected itself to the rule of law or allowed public debate on the national destiny. And in support of this system of government with no democratic limits on power, a primary weapon used by Swaziland's rulers has been to describe critics as 'foreign', divisive and hostile to Swazi 'tradition'.

During the lead-up to independence, King Sobhuza and his supporters had resisted the operation of political parties, already describing them as antithetical to the 'traditional' systems of Swazi government. Parties were formally allowed by the independence constitution, but in the pre-independence elections no opposition candidates won a seat. In the 1972 general elections, however, Swaziland's first as an independent country, an opposition political party, the Ngwane National Liberatory Congress (NNLC), gained three seats in parliament. The reaction was immediate. Before the elected candidates could be sworn in, the minister responsible for immigration issued a declaration that one of the members of the NNLC, Bhekindlela Thomas Ngwenya, was a 'prohibited immigrant' under the 1964 Immigration Act and subject to deportation.

Ngwenya challenged the declaration in court, and the deportation order was set aside by the High Court in August 1972 on the grounds that the government had not shown that he was not a citizen.[13] The government appealed.

While the appeal was pending, an amendment to the Immigration Act was rushed through parliament to establish a tribunal to decide cases of disputed nationality, from whose rulings an appeal could only be made to the Office of the Deputy Prime Minister, whose decision was final.[14] The tribunal, whose jurisdiction was retroactive, ruled that Ngwenya was not a citizen of Swaziland. Ngwenya then challenged the competence of the tribunal in the High Court, which ruled against him in January 1973;[15] on appeal, however, the Court of Appeal ruled in March 1973 that the amendment to the Immigration Act removing the jurisdiction of the High Court was unconstitutional because in effect it amounted to a constitutional amendment and had not followed the correct procedures.[16]

On 12 April 1973, the prime minister introduced a motion in parliament abrogating the constitution, the opposition walked out, and the king later that day announced the repeal of the constitution and then the banning of political parties.[17] Among the laws subsequently promulgated was an exceptionally exclusive 1974 citizenship law which essentially required applicants to show that they owed allegiance to a Swazi chief (*ukukhonta*) if they wished to acquire Swazi citizenship; part of a general rise in the political mobilization of Swazi ethnicity.[18]

In more recent years, the Swazi government has consistently

harassed Jan Sithole, the vocal general secretary of the Swaziland Federation of Trade Unions (SFTU). Among the many campaigns waged against Sithole for his outspokenness, which have included beatings and assault by security forces, court actions and kidnapping, has been an attack on his integrity and loyalty to Swaziland by virtue of his being a 'foreigner'. The authorities have claimed that Jan Sithole had no right to Swazi citizenship because his father came from Mozambique, despite the fact that he was born in Swaziland, had lived there all his life, and had a Swazi mother. Sithole had applied for citizenship in 1979 in order to comply with the 1974 legal requirements and had received no response. Subsequently, under a 1992 citizenship law, a right to Swazi nationality was conferred on persons whose mother but not father was a Swazi; but all such persons were required to seek a certificate of naturalization from the minister of home affairs.

In early June 1995, during a period of mass trade union mobilization and national stay-aways, Sithole was served with a notice ordering him to appear before a Citizenship Board to justify his claim to Swazi citizenship. Though the hearing never took place, on 19 July the authorities wrote to him asking for 'convincing proof' that he qualified as a citizen of Swaziland. Towards the end of 1995, the authorities also began investigating the citizenship status of Richard Nxumalo, the SFTU president, claiming that he was a South African.[19] Sithole and other trade union leaders faced constant surveillance, repeated arrests and multiple court cases during the same period and for many years thereafter. The citizenship allegations were one part of a more general pattern of harassment; and also part of a pattern in which those who criticized the government have been accused of being 'un-Swazi' for objecting to the style of rule by their traditional leader and absolute monarch, the Swazi king.

This pattern has continued. In late 2002, all six members of the Swaziland Court of Appeal (all South African citizens) resigned en masse, in protest at the royal family's explicit refusal to abide by two high-profile rulings the court had given; members of the legal profession went on strike in support of the judges.

In April 2003, several days after the International Bar Association issued a damning report on these events and the rule of law in Swaziland, Attorney General Phesheya Dlamini announced that the government had opened a file on prominent lawyers and others with dual citizenship, as part of a general crackdown on alleged improper conduct in the legal profession in the interests of 'the security of the country and its institutions'. Justifying this policy in the Senate, Minister of Home Affairs Prince Sobandla asserted – without legal basis – that dual citizenship in the kingdom was not allowed. Among those threatened with deportation was Paul Shilubane, president of the Swaziland Law Society and a vocal critic of the government, on the grounds that he had dual citizenship in South Africa.[20]

The current 2005 constitution creates a preference in favour of those 'generally regarded as Swazi by descent'. Meanwhile, among the provisions of the 1992 Citizenship Act, which is still in force, remains the possibility of acquiring citizenship 'by ukukhonta'; that is, under customary law. Though other ways of qualifying for citizenship are also now possible in theory, in practice those who are not ethnic Swazis find it very difficult to obtain recognition of citizenship. The 2005 constitution also explicitly confirms that a child born after the constitution came into force is a citizen only if his or her father is a citizen, one of the few recently adopted African constitutions to reaffirm gender inequality.[21]

Tanzania: attempts to silence the media

Tanzania has attempted to strip troublesome individuals of their citizenship several times in recent years. In 2001, the government declared that four individuals were not citizens, though giving them the option of applying for naturalization. The four were the country's then high commissioner to Nigeria, Timothy Bandora; Jenerali Ulimwengu (a leading publisher, journalist, media proprietor and chief executive of Habari Media Limited, and also a former Tanzanian diplomat and member of parliament, who was born and educated in Tanzania); Anatoli Amani (the leader of the ruling Chama Cha Mapinduzi – CCM – party in the north-western Kagera region); and Mouldine Castico (a former publicity secretary of CCM in Zanzibar). The declaration was interpreted as reprisal for independent coverage by Ulimwengu's media group of political and economic developments in Tanzania.[22]

In August 2006, the government of Tanzania again stripped two journalists of nationality, Ali Mohammed Nabwa, weekly consulting editor of *Fahamu*, and Mr Richard Mgamba, a reporter with the Mwanza-based *Citizen* newspaper. They were accused of being 'unpatriotic and enemies of the state'. The Zanzibar Immigration Department's revocation of Nabwa's citizenship came just days after his citizenship had been restored following a previous withdrawal when the Zanzibar government banned another newspaper he was heading as managing editor.[23]

Abuse of immigration law to silence non-citizens

African governments have also abused immigration law to silence critics among the long-term residents of their countries. Non-citizens have far fewer protections under international law than citizens, and immigration law is routinely administered in a fairly arbitrary way across the globe. Nevertheless, due-process protections apply just as much as they do to citizens: any deportee should have the right to challenge his or her deportation. Moreover, when non-citizens are long-term residents – and especially when their lack of citizenship is due to deficiencies in the systems for naturalization – use of immigration law against them has disturbing similarities to the attempts to denationalize those whose citizenship the government states is in doubt. Laws in many African countries, as in the cases from Zambia and Botswana described below, provide ample scope for removing non-citizens as a form of censorship.

Zambian law, like the law of many other African countries, gives the executive a very wide discretion to deport people if 'in the opinion of the minister' a person is 'likely to be a danger to peace or good order'.[24] This power has been invoked on many occasions and the courts have until recently mostly been very deferential in challenging executive discretion in these cases.[25] Some of those affected by this arbitrary action are long-term residents who have made the country their home: in 1994, for example, the minister of home affairs issued a deportation order against an Indian man married in Zambia to a Zambian woman and with two daughters in Zambia, and declared his presence in Zambia to be a danger to peace and good order. The courts followed precedent and refused to challenge the minister's decision.[26]

In a much more recent case, however, the Supreme Court did finally take a decision that placed some limits on ministerial power, ruling against the deportation of Roy Clarke, a British-born writer who has lived in Zambia for three decades, married a Zambian woman, with Zambian children and grandchildren – but had not become a Zambian citizen because Zambian citizenship law does not allow a woman to pass her citizenship to her husband.

On 1 January 2004, Clarke's regular column in Zambia's *Post* newspaper consisted of satirical comment on the president and two cabinet ministers. In Zambia, libelling the president is a criminal offence. The minister for home affairs signed a warrant for Clarke's deportation on 3 January, and announced the decision in an address to ruling party supporters on 5 January, saying that Clarke would be deported within twenty-four hours. Clarke filed an application for judicial review. Courageously, the High Court judge quashed the decision of the minister, saying it violated constitutional freedom of expression as well as procedural rules.[27] The state appealed, and in January 2008 the Supreme Court ruled against the government to hold that deportation was a disproportionate response to the offence caused by the article (though the judgment was based on far more limited grounds than the High Court ruling).[28]

A very similar case was unfolding in Botswana around the same time. In February 2005, Kenneth Good, a seventy-two-year-old Australian lecturer at the University of Botswana, resident in the country for fifteen years, was declared a prohibited immigrant as

Excluding candidates

an 'undesirable inhabitant' of Botswana and served with deportation papers for his immediate removal.[29] No official reason was given, but Good had been critical of the government; shortly after being declared prohibited he presented a paper at the university on 'Presidential succession in Botswana: no model for Africa'. Good challenged the deportation order in court. Papers filed on behalf of the president refused to give reasons as to why Good should be an undesirable inhabitant of Botswana.

After hearing the merits of case, the High Court ruled for the state in May 2005. Immediately the judgment was handed down, Good was arrested and put on a plane to South Africa. He appealed the decision from outside the country. In July 2005, the Court of Appeal, in a 4–1 decision, ruled that President Mogae did not act improperly and that the declaration of Professor Good as a prohibited immigrant was valid. In reaching this decision, the court ruled that Botswana's obligations under international law are secondary to the domestic laws of Botswana, and not binding until brought into national law by parliament. Thus, '[The President's] reasons for such a decision should neither be open to public disclosure nor be the subject of scrutiny by the courts.'[30] Good took his case to the African Commission, where a decision was pending as of late 2008.

8 | Naturalization and long-term integration

One of the principal problems facing long-term migrants to and within Africa, whether voluntary or involuntary, is the lack of effective procedures to give them a permanent legal status in their new country; that is, the lack of procedures to grant them citizenship. Whereas most African countries permit, in principle, the acquisition of citizenship by naturalization, in practice naturalization may be almost impossible to obtain.

The criteria on which citizenship by naturalization may be granted vary, but usually include long-term residence or marriage to a citizen. In some countries, acquiring citizenship by naturalization is relatively straightforward, at least in theory. More than twenty countries provide for a right to naturalize based on legal residence of five years; for others, the period required is up to fifteen or twenty years (Chad, Nigeria, Sierra Leone, Uganda) – or as much as thirty-five years for the Central African Republic. In many countries, marriage to a citizen either entitles one directly to citizenship, or reduces the residence period and other qualifications required for naturalization. South Africa provides a two-step process: a person must first become a permanent resident, a process that takes a minimum five years; following acquisition of permanent residence, a further five years' residence are required to become a citizen.

Though statistics are often hard to come by, those that are reported reveal that the numbers of those naturalized vary hugely across countries: more than 24,671 became naturalized citizens of South Africa during 2006/07 alone, with others resuming citizenship or registering citizenship by descent;[1] in Senegal, 12,000 people have been naturalized since independence in 1960.[2] Almost 6,000 foreigners have become Swazi citizens since independence, from almost 20,000 who applied.[3] Botswana granted 39,000 people citizenship between 1966 and 2004.[4] In Côte d'Ivoire, the 1998 census revealed that only 1 per cent of the population was naturalized and around a quarter was identified as of foreign origin.

Other countries apply much stricter rules, often designed to make it more difficult for those who are not 'natives' of the country to obtain citizenship. In many countries investigations are required, including interviews and police enquiries. Under the exceptionally demanding 2004 nationality law adopted by the Democratic Republic of Congo (DRC), applications for naturalization must be considered by the Council of Ministers and submitted to the National Assembly before being awarded by presidential decree; moreover, the individual must have rendered 'distinguished service' (*d'éminents services*) or provide a visible benefit to the country. In Sierra Leone, citizenship by naturalization is in theory possible after an (already long) fifteen-year legal residence period; in practice it is nearly impossible to obtain. According to available records (many were destroyed during the war) there are fewer than two hundred naturalized citizens. In Egypt naturalization is almost never granted, except to those born in Egypt, with a father of Egyptian origin or from an Arab or Muslim country. Although the grant of a presidential decree is common in civil-law countries and is often a routine administrative procedure without a heavy political weight, the requirement leaves a great deal of discretionary power in the executive branch.

Similarly, some countries apply criteria to naturalization based on cultural assimilation in addition to requirements of legal residence, in particular knowledge of the national language(s). At the most extreme, Ethiopia's 1930 Nationality Law, before it was repealed, required an applicant to 'know Amharic language perfectly, speaking and writing it fluently'. (The 2003 Proclamation on Ethiopian Nationality has reduced this requirement to an ability to 'communicate in any one of the languages of the nations/nationalities of the Country'.) While other countries have more manageable language and cultural requirements, these laws may be used in practice to restrict citizenship on an ethnic basis. Among the groups most seriously affected by deficiencies in laws for naturalization are refugees.

Refugees denied a permanent home

In the language used by the office of the UN High Commissioner for Refugees (UNHCR), there are three 'durable solutions' to the situation of individuals who have crossed an international border seeking refuge from persecution or from civil war: voluntary repatriation, local integration in the country of first asylum, or resettlement in a third country. Although voluntary repatriation to their home country is often the best outcome for those who have fled persecution or war, the reality is that for many repatriation may not be possible because of continued insecurity. Resettlement in a third country is only ever going to be possible for a small minority of those affected. Integration and permanent settlement in the country of refuge may therefore be needed, and the UN Convention on Refugees requires states to 'facilitate the assimilation and naturalization of refugees'; yet, even where refugees make progress in terms of economic and social integration, there are often no possibilities of converting refugee status into permanent residence and citizenship. As UNHCR puts it, with restraint: 'Progress has been rather modest in terms of local integration throughout the continent.'[5]

The record of African countries in providing citizenship to long-term refugee populations varies greatly, and many countries do not have laws that establish effective procedures for the acquisition of permanent residence and citizenship by refugees – or any other applicant.

Even in countries that have recently adopted refugee laws, they stop short of following the UN Refugee Convention's rules when it comes to providing for naturalization of refugee populations. For example, Uganda adopted a new Citizenship and Immigration Control Act in 1999 and a Refugees Act in 2006. In relation to naturalization, the Refugees Act simply states that 'the Constitution and any other law in force in Uganda shall apply to the naturalisation of a recognised refugee'. These laws require twenty years' residence in the country: an extremely long period for a refugee who may be able to claim the protection of no other country. Moreover, children born in the country to non-citizens can apply for registration as citizens – but children of refugees, perhaps the category most likely to need this right, are explicitly excluded by the constitution itself. In practice, administration of the immigration directorate has been poor, leading to vast backlogs of citizenship applications.

New refugee laws adopted in Kenya and Sierra Leone also do not grant any right to naturalize; even though the Sierra Leonean act provided for the 'facilitation of lasting solutions' and local integration of refugees. In practice, Kenya excludes refugees from the naturalization provisions of its general laws.

Egypt, like Kenya, does not offer refugees permanent residence or citizenship rights: the Egyptian government treats the position of refugees as temporary, allowing only two solutions – repatriation or resettlement in a third country. There is no specific refugee law, and though the constitution recognizes the concept of political refugee, this status has been granted only to a few high-profile individuals. For the rest, Egypt has effectively passed on the execution of its obligations under the UN Refugee Convention to the UNHCR Cairo office.[6] Moreover, Egypt instituted reservations to its ratification of the international instruments, relating to refugees' access to employment, state education and public relief and assistance or rationing. Refugees in Egypt and their children find it near impossible to obtain Egyptian nationality, unless they are married to or have a parent who is an Egyptian citizen; they do not qualify for naturalization as Egyptians regardless of the length of their residence in the country. Palestinian refugees in Egypt, who make up some 70,000 of the total 100,000 refugees and asylum seekers in the country, are particularly badly affected. Though they are to some extent integrated in Egyptian society and have preferential treatment with regard to accessing work, they are completely excluded from the possibility of obtaining citizenship, thanks to a 1959 decision of the Arab League that the Palestinian diaspora should not be given citizenship in other

> ### 'Participatory research' on refugee issues in Egypt
>
> Throughout my time doing research on Palestinian refugees in Egypt, I experienced interference from the Egyptian security authorities. This has now culminated in being held at Cairo airport when on the way from my home in Amman, Jordan to present a paper in Cairo on the unprotected Palestinians in Egypt. Later I was refused entry to Egypt and deported ...
>
> Of the many people who were in the waiting room, [one case] drew my attention: A Palestinian, holding an Egyptian travel document, was denied entry to Egypt since he overstayed his return visa. His mother is Egyptian and he was raised in Egypt where he remained until 15 years ago when he decided to leave and look for work elsewhere. Today, he works in Tanzania and was hoping to spend his holidays with his family in Cairo. The Egyptian authorities, denying him entry, told him to seek a visa for another country. Through contacts of his wife, he was waiting for a visa from Russia. He was not sure when he would leave, but he had hopes of receiving his visa in another five days.[7]

Arab countries, as a way of preserving their identity and political cause. Thus reforms adopted in 2004, which for the first time allowed the children of Egyptian women and foreign men to obtain nationality,[8] do not apply to those born of Palestinian fathers and Egyptian mothers. In practice, few if any children born to a Palestinian father and Egyptian mother have yet been granted citizenship, despite the change in the law.

There is, however, movement in the direction of improving access to citizenship by refugees in some other countries. Ghana allows for refugees to naturalize, though again studies of long-term Liberian refugees in Ghana showed they had many difficulties in claiming citizenship. In November 2006 it was reported that the Botswana president had approved the grant

Naturalization and integration

145

of citizenship to 183 long-term Angolan refugees resident in Botswana since the 1970s who had not repatriated to Angola at the end of the civil war there. Tanzania has a relatively good record on refugee status, including provision of citizenship in the 1990s to Rwandan refugees dating from the late 1950s and early 1960s, and, more recently, to several thousand Somali refugees in the north-eastern part of Tanzania. In 2007, Tanzania offered citizenship to almost 200,000 Burundian refugees resident in the

---

The story of Khoti Chilomba Kamanga

In 1980, I was leading a fairly a comfortable life for a twenty-two-year-old, single and working as a personnel assistant at the American embassy in Lilongwe. But the political climate in Malawi was suffocating and highly dangerous. I joined the League for a Socialist Malawi (LESOMA), whose leader, Dr Attati Mpakati, was to be shot dead in Harare by agents of the Malawian government. When it became too risky to remain in the country, I opted to flee to Tanzania and became a refugee. Little did I know that, like many exiled compatriots, my grandparents, both parents, as well as a sister, would die without my participation in the burial rituals.

But I wasn't fleeing to a strange land. My parents had, in March 1933, come to what was then Tanganyika (present-day Tanzania) as migrant workers from Nyasaland (now Malawi), my father working initially as a railway stationmaster and retiring from the Tanzania civil service. I was born in the railway town of Shinyanga, and enjoyed my early childhood and education in Dar es Salaam.

I arrived back in Dar es Salaam on 28 July 1980, on a regular commercial flight. A Tanzanian government Aliens Travel Document (ATD No. 5890) was issued to me on 6 August 1980. Humbling hospitality, astonishing efficiency.

From Dar es Salaam, I travelled to Moscow and joined

the Patrice Lumumba University. I mastered the Russian language, began enjoying the food and learned to cope with the long, harsh winters. Eleven years elapsed before I left Moscow to return to Africa. While I was in Moscow, the Tanzanian government replaced the ATD in my possession with the more respectable-looking and widely recognized Nansen passport. On its face were emblazoned the words: 'UN Convention of 28 July 1951 Travel Document'. And with this new international identification document it became possible for the first time to visit countries that had never recognized the ATD.

On return to Dar es Salaam in 1991, one of my first calls was on the Refugee Unit of the Ministry of Home Affairs. Once again, I was speedily issued a document which is among my most treasured. The University of Dar es Salaam had already indicated they would offer me a job if I would produce a work permit. Written in Kiswahili, the Home Affairs permit recognized that I was a refugee and contained the following magic words: 'This document serves as authorization for him to be offered a job or be in gainful employment.' I was able to take the promised work at the university, and soon became the director there of the Centre for the Study of Forced Migration.

When did I cease to be a refugee?

Following the collapse of the Banda regime in 1994 and the advent of democratic rule in Malawi, Tanzania applied the 'cessation clause' in the Refugee Convention. I would no longer be entitled to the Nansen passport, the only valid travelling document in my possession. There was the option of quitting my job and returning to Malawi, a country in which I had not lived since fleeing in 1980. Remaining in Tanzania, the country of my birth and residence for the last three years, seemed more sensible. But it wouldn't be that simple.

I rushed to Malawi to obtain a passport, which I did in June

1995. With that, I returned to the Tanzanian immigration authorities to have my residence status restored and thus keep my job. I had solved one major problem. But not the anxieties of seeking contract renewals nor going in and out of the immigration to sort out my residence permit.

My naturalization application form bears the date 18 January 1998. As early as 14 February 2000 I swore the 'Oath of Allegiance' to the Republic of Tanzania, vowing to preserve, protect and defend the constitution; and yet for the next four years was allowed to continue holding only an alien passport.

A naturalization certificate was issued on April Fool's Day of 2004, but to obtain a Tanzanian passport I had also to furnish evidence of renunciation of Malawian citizenship. The Malawian consular authorities in Dar es Salaam advised me to please travel to Malawi and handle this matter in person. In Blantyre for the purpose, I was welcomed warmly, if quizzically. But once I had handed over the Malawi passport in return for the renunciation certificate, I remained without a valid travel document to allow me to re-enter Tanzania! After much head-scratching by the authorities, it was decided that an 'Alien's Emergency Certificate' would be issued. The reasoning was articulated in the following fashion: 'The bearer has renounced Malawi citizenship and now is a Tanzania [*sic*]. This is to enable him travel to Tanzania as he has no passport at the moment.'[10]

country since 1972 and their descendants. But these examples are too few and far between and leave too many excluded.[9]

In South Africa, the years after the transition to democratic rule saw a wholesale review of the treatment of refugees. The new government immediately ratified the refugee conventions and, even before legislative changes to the immigration regime were passed, offered a series of immigration amnesties to particular groups of foreigners from the region: contract mineworkers (1995); a broader category of people from the SADC region who had lived in South Africa for at least five years and had economic or family ties in the country (1996); and finally Mozambicans displaced by the civil war in that country who had been refused refugee status by the apartheid government (1999).[11] An estimated 1–1.5 million people became eligible for South African citizenship in this way, though only 51,000 applications were received from miners, and just over 200,000 for others from the SADC region.[12]

Included within the flood of reforming legislation adopted by the post-apartheid government during its first decade were new refugee and immigration laws.[13] These laws drew a clear distinction between asylum seekers and refugees and other migrants, and a bureaucratic apparatus was established to deal with applications for refugee status. Around a quarter of a million people have applied for and more than thirty thousand have been granted refugee status, though there are vast backlogs and acknowledged refugees may still struggle to gain the necessary identity documents that should follow.[14] Despite difficulties in practice, South Africa's system does, notably, provide for a transfer of status from refugee to permanent residence and then naturalized citizenship. After five years of continuous residence in South Africa from the date that asylum was granted, the Immigration Act allows for the granting of (permanent) residence to a refugee if the Standing Committee for Refugee Affairs provides a certificate that he or she will remain a refugee indefinitely. Five years after that, a permanent resident can apply for citizenship by the usual rules.

Moreover, of the extensive list of rights in the South African constitution, including comprehensive socio-economic rights, only four rights are limited to citizens: the citizenship right itself, political rights (to vote and stand for office), the right to residence, and rights to freedom of trade, occupation and profession. The courts have confirmed that all others are applicable to non-citizens, and arguably to all non-nationals (including those who are not legally present in the country).[15]

South Africa also illustrates, of course, the limits of legal definitions. From the mid-1990s, as South Africa's borders opened up to the continent, increasing numbers of migrants and refugees came to the country. The numbers of undocumented migrants are highly contested, but probably run to the millions, swelled in recent years by Zimbabweans desperate for work in a functioning economy. But national human rights organizations reported ever more serious worries about xenophobia among the native South African population towards these incomers. In May and June 2008, the situation radically worsened, when attacks on foreigners broke out in Johannesburg, Cape Town and other urban centres, leaving more than sixty dead and displacing tens of thousands.

Tangled up with the resentment and competition for resources that led to violence was the strong sense of ordinary, poor, South Africans that they have been excluded from the great wealth of the country, despite the transition of 1994, and often overtaken by the newcomers. Apparently endemic corruption among officials of the Department of Home Affairs and police means that even those who do hold South African national documents may not be believed. More than a quarter of South Africans want a total ban on immigration. Yet hostile feelings are more complex than a generalized resentment of foreigners, being moderated by race, gender, ethnicity and economic status.[16] Somehow, it seems that South Africa's history of pass laws and population control still has a grip on the popular imagination; while the ANC government's failure to deliver constitutionally promised rights has fuelled tensions not only between citizens and non-citizens but also among different (racial) categories of citizens. A commitment to non-discrimination in citizenship and other law is not enough to solve these problems, which will need a much wider range of policy responses. Yet a continuing official commitment to non-discrimination can also send a signal of societal values that can in time have a much broader effect.

In general, the countries that deal most effectively and humanely with long-term refugees are those with the most liberal naturalization regimes, in which special measures for naturaliza-

Former President Mbeki on migration and xenophobia

Apart from anything else, our intimate relationship with the rest of our Continent is illustrated by the significant numbers of fellow Africans who have sought to settle in South Africa since 1994. Undoubtedly, this trend will continue, adding a new richness to our own society.

Many of these new immigrants bring with them important skills that our country needs. Many of them are also people who are creative, full of initiative and driven by an enterprising spirit. The more they impart these characteristics to us as well, the better we will be as a people and a society.

Necessarily, we must continue to be vigilant against any evidence of xenophobia against the African immigrants. It is fundamentally wrong and unacceptable that we should treat people who come to us as friends as though they are our enemies. We should also never forget that the same peoples welcomed us to their own countries when many of our citizens had to go into exile as a result of the brutality of the apartheid system.

To express the critical importance of Africa to ourselves, both black and white, we should say that we are either African or we are nothing. We can only succeed in the objectives we pursue if the rest of our Continent also succeeds. We sink or swim together.

ANC Today: Letter from the State President, 1(18), 25 May 2001

tion of refugees are not required because length of residence is the critical criterion. The law in these countries sets the mood for an inclusive and generous incorporation of new members of the society.

Senegal, for example, provides that anyone from a neighbouring country (from which refugees are most likely to come) who has lived in the country for five years can simply opt for Senegalese nationality, without further conditions. Although many of the more than 60,000 Mauritanians expelled from their country in 1989/90 who became refugees in Senegal resisted taking Senegalese citizenship because they feared losing their claim to Mauritanian citizenship, many did do so to facilitate travel and work, even if they preferred not to admit this publicly. Senegal promised that it would guarantee citizenship to any Mauritanians who chose not to return following the invitation to do so in 2007.

Western Sahara, Morocco and Algeria: Sahrawi refugees stateless for three decades

The Western Saharan refugees in Algeria constitute one of the largest and longest-standing populations of unintegrated refugees in Africa. Though in a less extreme way than the Palestinians, they are trapped in a citizenship black hole, thanks to a political failure to resolve the fundamental questions of state existence that first led to their flight. Those who remained in their homes in Western Sahara and oppose Morocco's de facto control of the territory face significant restrictions on their civil liberties, including in some cases the right to identity papers and travel documents.

Western Sahara is a former Spanish territory on the western edge of North Africa, bordered by Morocco, Algeria and Mauritania. Its status has been disputed between the Kingdom of Morocco and the Polisario Front[17] independence movement for more than thirty years. While this dispute has remained unresolved, with Morocco in occupation of the territory, more than 150,000 Western Saharans, known as Sahrawis, have lived as stateless refugees in Algeria.

The territory was declared a Spanish colonial protectorate in 1884; in 1958 its legal status was changed under Spanish law so that it became an autonomous province with a degree of elected self-government, whose residents were Spanish nationals. A liberation movement emerged in the 1960s and 1970s and a series of UN resolutions called on Spain to hold a referendum on self-determination for Western Sahara, but only in 1974 did Spain concede the principle of a referendum and begin compiling a census of the population. King Hassan II of Morocco, however, announced that Morocco would not accept a referendum that included an option for independence; Mauritania also claimed the territory. At the request of Morocco, the UN General Assembly referred the situation to the International Court of Justice for an advisory opinion: in October 1975, the ICJ ruled that neither Morocco nor Mauritania had any legal claim over Western Saharan territory.

Just days after the ICJ ruling, Moroccan armed forces crossed the border and occupied most of the northern part of the Western Sahara territory, followed by a 'green march' of several hundred thousand Moroccan civilians to 'reclaim' the region for Morocco. Spain then signed an agreement in Madrid with Morocco and Mauritania which agreed a temporary tripartite administration of the territory; in April 1976, Morocco and Mauritania subsequently agreed a partition between just their two states. Meanwhile, Polisario proclaimed the creation of the Sahrawi Arab Democratic Republic (SADR) on 27 February 1976, following Spain's formal withdrawal the day before. Mauritania renounced its claims to the territory in 1979 and withdrew its forces, following losses in fighting with Polisario; but Moroccan forces remain until today in occupation of most of the former Spanish colony, with only a small strip in the east under the control of Polisario/SADR.

As a result of the Moroccan takeover, around half of the native population fled the territory: by mid-1976 there were 40,000 refugees, growing to 80,000 by the end of 1977. According to the government of Algeria, it hosts today an estimated 165,000 Sahrawi refugees, though the number is contested.[18] Most of these people are still in four camps near Tindouf, a historic oasis town in southern Algeria. Though the camps are poor, the Sahrawi refugees have access to some health, education and other services, thanks to infrastructure established by Polisario with support from the UN, the European Union and other countries, as well as solidarity groups in Spain and elsewhere. Initial close control of the camps by Polisario has opened up to a somewhat freer system; and, though the Polisario and Algerian authorities have checkpoints on the roads leaving the camps, including to the border posts, in practice camp residents seem to be largely free to leave on trips of short or longer duration. Travel within Algeria beyond Tindouf, however, may require permission from the Algerian authorities.[19]

A UN-sponsored ceasefire was agreed between Morocco and Polisario in 1991, based on a peace plan that provided for the establishment of a United Nations mission (known as MINURSO) to organize a referendum on independence or other status for the territory.[20] To date, no referendum has been held. Among the key points of contention are the eligibility criteria to vote in the referendum, the options available to be voted for, and the return of refugees from Algeria. Morocco has continued to put forward proposals by which Western Sahara would remain within its control, but with some level of devolution of power to locally elected bodies and officials. In January 2000, after interviewing almost 200,000 applicants, the Identification Commission of MINURSO published a list of just over 86,000 persons eligible to vote in the referendum (48,000 living under Moroccan control and 38,000 in the refugee camps), based on the Spanish census of 1974; Morocco, however, lodged more than 120,000 appeals on behalf of the settler population in the territory. UNHCR also prepared an unpublished list of refugees to be repatriated. The total population in the area under Moroccan control is today close to 400,000.[21] In 2007, Morocco presented a new plan for Western Saharan autonomy to the UN.

In 1984, the support of Algeria and (at that time) Libya won the SADR recognition from the Organization of African Unity (OAU), following the failure of OAU peace brokering efforts to reach a successful conclusion. Morocco then withdrew from membership of the continental body.[22] Algeria remains the SADR/Polisario's main supporter. At different times, more than seventy states have recognized the SADR, most of them in Africa and Latin America, though in more recent years several African countries have cancelled or 'suspended' their recognition, following the latest Moroccan offer of a form of autonomy to the territory – and Moroccan incentives for a change of position. As of late 2008, the total number of countries recognizing the republic was just over forty.[23] Morocco has never been recognized as the 'administering power' of the territory by the United Nations under the legal framework providing for 'non-self-governing territories'.[24]

The SADR issues national identity cards to Sahrawis living in the refugee camps and the territories under SADR control, and those who wish to travel abroad are granted Sahrawi passports, with which they can travel to the few countries recognizing the Sahrawi Republic, including Mauritania. The government of Algeria issues short-term passports to Sahrawi refugees who need to travel – usually for reasons of medical treatment, family unification, and so on – to countries that do not recognize the SADR. These passports are obtained by applying to the Algerian authorities via the SADR bureaucracy, but are only travel documents and do not imply recognition of the refugees as Algerian citizens.[25] Group permit schemes also allow many thousands of Sahrawi children to travel each year to Spain, Venezuela, Cuba, Italy and other countries to be hosted by families offering solidarity with the refugees. An unknown number of Sahrawis also have citizenship in Mauritania, where many have family or other ties.

In 1976, Spain adopted a decree giving natives of former Spanish Sahara the option during a period of one year to opt for Spanish nationality, under certain conditions.[26] Because of the nature of the Western Sahara legal status, however – in which the International Court of Justice rejected Morocco's claim to any legal tie to the territory, while the UN does not recognize Morocco as the administering power – the general principle of an individual choice in case of succession of states between the nationality of predecessor or successor state does not apply.

Nevertheless, those Sahrawis living in the area under Moroccan occupation are under Moroccan law Moroccan nationals eligible for travel and other documentation; moreover, the Moroccan nationality code does not allow for an individual to renounce

Moroccan citizenship except as authorized by decree.[27] Since 1977, the inhabitants of the Western Saharan territories occupied by Morocco have also been able to participate in Moroccan national and regional elections. Many Sahrawis, however, reject Moroccan nationality and continue to protest against Moroccan administration of the territory; there were new waves of protest in 1999 and 2005.

In practice, civil liberties are still restricted in Moroccan-administered Western Sahara, though the human rights situation has greatly improved in recent years. Many Sahrawis were among the hundreds of 'disappearances' that took place in Morocco from the mid-1960s to the early 1990s. Moroccan legislation prohibits attacks on the kingdom's 'territorial integrity', and activists for Western Saharan independence still face harassment, including deprivation of travel and nationality documents.[28] For example, Brahim Sabbar, a human rights activist documenting violations in Western Sahara, spent a decade in prison in the 1980s, and from 2000 to at least 2007 was denied a passport.[29] A group of Sahrawis were deprived of their passports for several years after they attempted to travel to Geneva to participate in UN human rights activities in 2003, though they have since been permitted to travel again.[30] More recently, Sahrawi activists employed in civil service jobs have been refused permission by their employers to take leave in order to travel.

A satisfactory resolution of the Sahrawis' plight may have to wait for a political settlement. But in the meantime, the political bargaining should not prevent them from obtaining the citizenship of the countries where they find themselves, especially Algeria, under the normal processes of naturalization available under Algerian law.

9 | Last words: before Africa can unite?

In 1963, just as the Organization of African Unity was being founded by Africa's newly independent states, President Kwame Nkrumah of Ghana published his book *Africa Must Unite*. Nkrumah, the leader of the first sub-Saharan African country to gain independence from its former colonial power, called for the speedy political union of the whole continent: 'Seek ye first the political kingdom, and all else shall be added unto you.'

Nkrumah's vision did not carry the day. Though Ghana was supported during the negotiations to establish the OAU by the North African countries Algeria, Egypt, Libya and Morocco, as well as Guinea and Mali (collectively known as the 'Casablanca Group'), it was decided that colonial borders would be respected.[1] Other leaders of newly independent African states did not see the merit of giving up their hard-won powers to a continental federation, preferring the 'step by step' approach to African unity proposed by President Julius Nyerere of Tanzania (and the much larger 'Monrovia Group' of states).

In the years following 1963, African states largely concentrated on their own internal problems and on the effort to free the remaining colonies or white-minority regimes from European rule. The project to build Africa-wide political structures and an African citizenship was put on hold. Already established regional political unions collapsed; including Nkrumah's own Ghana–Mali–Guinea union, and the East African federation of Kenya, Uganda and Tanzania.

Nevertheless, the pan-African ideal kept its powerful appeal across the African continent. African leaders through the decades that followed have echoed Nkrumah's sentiments, whether or not they are keen supporters of the political project. Even former South African president Thabo Mbeki, one of the more cautious leaders on the subject of continental political integration, chose to open and thread his speech at the symbolic moment of adoption of South Africa's post-apartheid constitution in 1996 with the words 'I am an African'. Ordinary Africans are perhaps more likely to identify with an idea of 'Africa' than Europeans with an idea of 'Europe'.

In the last decade, the debate over pan-Africanism and the idea of continental political union has acquired new urgency. The end of the cold war, the final achievement of majority rule in South Africa, and the rapidly accumulating pressures of economic globalization all played a part in the revival: all three developments created new possibilities and new needs for Africa to speak with one voice. Libyan head of state Mu'ammer al Gaddafi was the unlikely catalyst for action. Gaddafi, rebuffed by Arab states in his efforts to become a regional political leader, turned to Africa for support and used Libya's oil wealth to back the initiative that put a new continental political framework in place. In September 1999, African heads of state and government meeting in Libya under the auspices of the OAU issued the 'Sirte Declaration' calling for the establishment of an African Union, in order to 'rekindle the aspirations of our peoples for stronger unity, solidarity and cohesion in a larger community of peoples transcending cultural, ideological, ethnic, and national differences'.

Thanks to the same divisions that had existed in the 1960s, the African Union that was eventually created in 2002 to replace the OAU aspires to an architecture more similar to that of the European Union than a close political federation. Further discussions from 2006 at head-of-state level on the route 'Towards a United States of Africa' have not resulted so far in any such grandiose outcomes; though fitful progress has been made at achieving greater subregional integration, including the revival of an East African Community and strengthening of cooperation elsewhere. In February 2009, Gaddafi was himself elected to serve a one-year term as chairperson of the AU, with promises to drive the process forward.

The debates surrounding these issues have also relaunched the discussion of a common African citizenship that had flourished decades earlier. In 2002, the year the new African Union was created, a high-level meeting adopted a consensus statement urging that 'Africa should move towards a common citizenship, through the initial steps of harmonizing citizenship, naturalization, immigration and employment laws, and through progressively removing restrictions on travel'.[2] In 2004 and 2005, further meetings endorsed the idea of an African passport.[3] In 2007, an African diplomatic passport was actually launched, for staff and representatives of the AU structures; a small step towards the longer-term aim.[4]

These proposals are not just an esoteric exercise for those who attend the apparently endless round of international meetings that seldom seem to have results in the real world; or at least they have the potential to be much more significant. A commitment to greater African integration and recognition of a common African destiny at continental level provide an important opening for the debate about citizenship rights. If each state in Africa has different and contradictory rules for the identification of its own citizens, how can there be common rules for being a citizen of the continent? If these rules are abusive of the rights of those who should by any rational system be citizens of each country, how can a continental citizenship be built that itself is something that Africa's peoples would aspire to and which would ensure them a brighter future? If there are millions of people who live in Africa and know no other home but are not recognized as citizens by any individual state, what hope can they have from a stronger continental government?

The current moment is a critical opportunity to begin the process of addressing these problems. The debate over the creation of a 'Union Government' for Africa draws on deep roots of the pan-African ideology that fundamentally rejects distinctions of culture, language and 'tribe', as well as colonial borders. And though some strands of pan-Africanism contain a strong racist element based on skin colour, many others do not, backing instead the concept of pan-Africanism as a political and not a racial or cultural project. But this 'grand debate' on continental unity is so far missing a serious discussion on the content of African citizenship laws today, and the need for their harmonization in line with principles of equality and non-discrimination before an African citizenship can be created. The case studies in this book show how much such a discussion is needed. With clear political leadership at continental and at national level to re-define the national community on an inclusive basis, histories of discrimination and violence can be overcome.

To solve these problems, African countries will need to move towards the international norm whereby legal citizenship is not based on ethnicity or inherited connection to the land, but rather on objective criteria that welcome as new members of the national community all those who can make a contribution to its future. The gender discrimination in the grant of citizenship that con-demns many to a half-life where they can never fully participate in community or national debates must be ended. Treating people as not 'authentic' citizens means that their loyalty to the state will indeed be tested; generosity to newcomers will inspire the stronger loyalty in return.

Of course, resolution of the complex problems of exclusion and inequality will require action across the board and not only reforms of citizenship law. Côte d'Ivoire, DRC and Zimbabwe most obviously – but also many other countries – will need equitable methods to adjudicate competing claims to land and provide secure tenure for the future. Everywhere measures are essential to ensure rights to access state services and to benefit on a more equal basis from the national wealth, whatever one's race, ethnicity, gender or region of residence. Measures of affirmative action are justified to overcome inequalities created by colonial history. In all African countries a greater respect for due process and the independence of the judiciary, limits on executive power and action against grand corruption, as well as better design of electoral systems and electoral management, must contribute towards the creation of states in which all can be sure that their rights will be respected without the need to take up arms. The education system can make its contribution to ensuring that individuals can engage with equal autonomy in both the public and private spheres.

But an effort to address citizenship-law discrimination will in the countries affected be at the centre of these efforts. African states, like other states, are made up of people thrown together by historical circumstance. A citizenship law that founds itself on a concept of ethnic or racial purity, or an essential link to the land, is not adapted to the reality of historical and contemporary migration. Those who find themselves living within a single polity on a lifetime basis need rules, fair rules, to govern their right to belong to that state. Systems that are not based on equal citizenship for all can only be disastrous. Countries that are not at ease with their existing populations will hardly be able to commit to an 'ever closer union' with neighbouring states.

Notes

1 Introduction

1 Benedict Anderson, *Imagined Communities: Reflections on the Origins and Spread of Nationalism* (London: Verso, 1991).

2 Mahmood Mamdani, *Citizen and Subject: Contemporary Africa and the Legacy of Late Colonialism*, (Princeton, NJ: Princeton University Press, 1986).

3 For a discussion on the use of the term 'tribe', see, Chris Lowe, 'Talking about "tribe": moving from stereotypes to analysis', *Africa Action*, updated version, February 2008, available at: www.africaaction.org//bp/ethall.htm.

2 Empire to independence

1 This summary of African citizenship law is based on a comprehensive comparative study published by the Open Society Institute, *Citizenship Law in Africa: A Comparative Study* (forthcoming, 2009), from which full references to the laws cited and further details can be obtained.

2 In the last few years of colonial rule, Portugal and France extended citizenship rights in the metropolitan territory to all in their colonies, but not on a completely equal basis.

3 Protocol to the African Charter on Human and Peoples' Rights on the Rights of Women in Africa, Article 6.

3 Natives and settlers

1 Constitution of Zimbabwe Amendment Act, No. 3 of 1983.

2 Citizenship of Zimbabwe Act, No. 23 of 1984.

3 Constitution of Zimbabwe (Amendment No. 11) Act, No. 30 of 1990, inserting Article 3(1)(b) to Schedule 3 of the constitution.

4 *Rattigan and others* v. *Chief Immigration Officer, Zimbabwe, and others*, 1995 (2) SA 182 (ZS).

5 'Mugabe tries to bar whites from Zim poll', AFP, 13 May 2000.

6 The registrar-general's office is responsible for maintaining the voters' roll and other aspects of elections, citizenship, passports, births, marriages and deaths, and for national population registration and the system of national identity cards.

7 'Court rules on Zimbabwe citizenship', AP, 1 December 2000; *Carr* v. *Registrar-General*, 2000 (2) ZLR 433 (S).

8 'Registrar-General loses citizenship case', *Daily News*, 17 January 2001.

9 Citizenship Amendment Act No. 12 of 2001, section 3(c), repealing section 9(7) of the

Citizenship of Zimbabwe Act, chapter 4:01, and substituting the text here. The amendment act also inserted a provision in Article 13 to revoke the citizenship of a person who is absent from the country for five years.

10 *Sunday Mail*, quoted in the *Zimbabwe Human Rights Bulletin*, Issue 5, Zimbabwe Lawyers for Human Rights, September 2001.

11 'Zim threatens to take away critics' passports', *The Star* (Johannesburg), 17 February 2001. Moyo later argued against just this position once he left ZANU-PF to become an independent MP. See Professor Jonathan Moyo, 'Constitutional madness will not save Zanu PF', NewZimbabwe.com, 26 August 2005.

12 'Citizenship law under scrutiny', *Zimbabwe Independent*, 19 October 2001.

13 'Zimbabwe loses second citizenship case', *The Star* (Johannesburg), 12 June 2002.

14 Zimbabwean Lawyers for Human Rights, 'Zimbabwe Lawyers for Human Rights submissions on the interpretation of citizenship laws to the Parliamentary Committee on Defence and Home Affairs', 7 March 2007, available at www.zlhr.org.zw/Citizenship/Citizenship%20submissions%20to%20committee.doc, accessed 28 November 2007.

15 *Petho* v. *Minister of Home Affairs, Zimbabwe and Another* (07/06/02) [2002] ZWSC 80; *ZWNews*, 9 March 2003.

16 *Tsvangirai* v. *Registrar-General and Others* (HC 12092/01) [2002] ZWHHC 29, 27 February 2002.

17 *Todd* v. *Registrar-General of Citizenship and Another* (HC 55/2002) [2002] ZWHHC 76, 7 May 2002.

18 'Zimbabwe loses second citizenship case', *The Star* (Johannesburg), 12 June 2002.

19 *Tsvangirai* v. *Registrar-General of Elections and Another*, *Tsvangirai* v. *Registrar-General of Elections and Others* (HC 11843/01, HC 12015/01) [2002] ZWHHC 22, 25 January 2002.

20 *Registrar-General of Elections and Others* v. *Tsvangirai* (30/2002) [2002] ZWSC 12, 28 February 2002.

21 *Peter Jackson and 634 Others* v. *Registrar-General* (HC 2434/02), 7 March 2002 (unreported).

22 Constitution of Zimbabwe Amendment Act (No. 17 of 2005), section 20(b), repealing schedule 3, Article 3(1)(b) of the constitution on 'Qualifications and disqualifications for voters'. See also 'Representations on the Bill Made by the Zimbabwe Human Rights NGO Forum to the Portfolio Committee on Justice, Legal and Parliamentary Affairs', 4 August 2005.

23 Judith Todd, 'When would-be heroes turn bad', *Mail & Guardian*, Johannesburg, 3 May 2007.

24 Basildon Peta, 'Zimbabwe strips former PM Smith of his citizenship', *Independent*, London, 28 March 2002.

25 General Notice 584 of 2002.

26 Fourth Report of the Portfolio Committee on Defence and Home Affairs on the Citizenship of Zimbabwe Act, 13 June 2007.

27 *Registrar-General of Citizenship* v. *Todd* (58/02/01) [2003] ZWSC 4, 27 February 2003.

28 *Job Sibanda* v. *Registrar-General of Citizenship and Other* (HH 3626/02); 'Man born of foreign parents is Zimbabwean – judge', *Legalbrief Today,* 20 June 2005.

29 'Zimbabwe Lawyers for Human Rights submissions on the interpretation of citizenship laws to the Parliamentary Committee on Defence and Home Affairs', 7 March 2007.

30 *Trevor Ncube* v. *Registrar-General* (HH 7316/06), 25 January 2007.

31 Citizenship of Zimbabwe Amendment Act, No. 12 of 2003, chapter 4, Article 9A(d).

32 Indigenization and Economic Empowerment Bill, 2007, preamble and Article 2.

33 Constitution of the Republic of Kenya, 1963, Articles 87 and 88; Constitution of the Republic of Uganda, 1962, Articles 7–12.

34 Constitution of the Republic of Kenya, 1963, Article 92; Constitution of the Republic of Uganda, 1962, Articles 7–12.

35 In Zanzibar also, as early as 1964, the government of the island deprived some seven thousand people of Asian descent of the Zanzibari citizenship they had chosen in preference to British.

See Rhoda E. Howard-Hassmann, *Human Rights in Commonwealth Africa*, Rowman and Littlefield, 1986, p. 102.

36 Kenya Citizenship Act, 1963, section 3(1)(b)(ii). The applicant or one of his parents must be born in a country to which the section applies, or have been resident in that country or Kenya for a period of five years. Further, he has to have adequate knowledge of Kiswahili or the English language, be of good character and a suitable citizen of Kenya. In practice, very few apply for citizenship under this provision. The 1963 constitution provided, in addition to the transitional provisions relating to acquisition of citizenship at independence, for citizenship by registration for Commonwealth citizens or citizens of another African country – but did not make reference to African descent.

37 Gibson Kamau Kuria, 'Is the Kenya Constitution colour blind? The Constitution and the Africanisation of the economy, with particular reference to Africanisation of commerce', n.d. According to information received from an immigration officer this provision has in fact never been used; telephone interview by Rose Ayugi, 2005.

38 Uganda Citizenship Ordinance (No. 63 of 1962).

39 Constitution of the Republic of Uganda, 1967, Article 4.

40 *Wadhwa and Others* v. *City Council of Nairobi* [1968] E.A. 406;

see also Alan H. Smith, 'Prevention of discrimination under Kenyan law', *International and Comparative Law Quarterly*, 20(1), January 1971, pp. 136–42.

41 The council argued that its resolution was not racially discriminatory since the term African should be taken to mean not a person whose forefathers were born in Africa but rather a citizen of any country on the continent of Africa, without regard to race. The judge rejected this line of argument on the grounds that the provisions on citizenship did not extend automatically to citizens of other countries in Africa, except as listed in the Citizenship Act. In a somewhat similar case heard before the Kenya High Court in 1968, *Fernandes* v. *Kericho Licensing Court*, the question of citizenship arose once again. The plaintiff was of Indian origin and was denied renewal of a liquor licence on the basis that he was not a citizen. The court found in favour of the plaintiff, on the grounds that under the relevant law (Liquor Licensing Act, Laws of Kenya, chapter 121) the liquor court had power to refuse to renew the applicant's licence only if he was suffering from one of the six disqualifications set out in the Act, and lack of citizenship was not one of them.

42 Patrick Keatly, 'Britain could face influx of 80,000 Asians', *Guardian* (London), 5 August 1972.

43 Immigration (Cancellation of Entry Permits and Certificates of Residence) Decree (No. 17 of 1972), 9 August 1972; Immigration (Cancellation of Entry Permits and Certificates of Residence) (Amendment) Decree (No. 30 of 1972), 25 October 1972.

44 Uganda Expropriated Properties Act, Laws of Uganda, 2000, chapter 87, transferred the properties and businesses of Asians that had been acquired or expropriated during the military regime to the Ministry of Finance and ensured their return to former owners or their lawful disposal by government.

45 The issue led to several court cases. In *Kayondo* v. *Asian Property Custodian Board* (HCCS No. 345 of 1981), the presiding judge stated that the seizure of businesses and other properties by the military government from Asians was unconstitutional. On appeal (HCB No. 17 of 1982), however, it was held that the takeover of the property amounted to nationalization and therefore was not a violation of the constitution. Some cases relating to ownership of formerly Asian-held properties took years to resolve; others continue to be fought out in the courts.

46 Evelyn Kwamboka and Juliet Otieno, 'Stateless man's agony after a year of life at the airport', *The Standard*, 15 June 2005; Adam Mynott, 'Kenya airport dweller is British', BBC News, 12 July 2005. In the 2004 film *The Terminal*, Tom Hanks played an immigrant trapped at JFK airport in New York in similar circumstances.

47 Uganda Constitutional Review Commission report, December 2003, p. 157, available from www.ugandaonlinelaw library.com/files/constitution/ Commission_of_Inquiry.PDF, accessed 20 November 2007.

48 Constitution of the Republic of Uganda, 1995, Article 10.

49 Constitution of the Republic of Uganda, 1995, third schedule; Uganda Constitution (Amendment) Act, 2005.

50 In Kenya, meanwhile, a draft constitution produced in 2002 after an extensive national consultation, but never formally adopted, moved in the other direction, removing gender discrimination and providing much due-process protection to all. *The People's Choice: The Report of the Constitution of Kenya Review Commission*, September 2002.

51 See Konia T. Kollehlon, 'On race, citizenship and property in Liberia', *The Perspective*, Atlanta, GA, 19 March 2008.

52 Constitution of Sierra Leone, 1961, section 1(1).

53 Sierra Leone Constitution (Amendment) (No. 2) Act, No. 12 of 1962, and Constitution (Amendment) (No. 3) Act, No. 39 of 1962.

54 Sierra Leone Constitution (Amendment) (No. 2) Act, No. 12 of 1962, section 2(b).

55 The Non-Citizens (Interests in Land) Act of 1966. The Sierra Leone Provinces Land Act, 1960, also made a distinction between 'natives' who were originally from the provinces and 'non-natives'

who were from the Western Area (where the capital, Freetown, is located). A native is defined in the Sierra Leone Citizenship Act of 1973 as follows: '"native" means a citizen of Sierra Leone who is a member of a race, tribe or community settled in Sierra Leone, other than a race, tribe or community: (a) which is of European or Asiatic or American origin; or (b) whose principal place of settlement is the Western Area'.

The Krios (descendants of various groups of freed slaves landed in Freetown in the eighteenth and nineteenth centuries and estimated to form about 3 per cent of the population today) and any person whose background cannot be traced to the provinces are 'non-natives'; 'natives' are those from a tribe or community from the provinces. This distinction continues to apply in Sierra Leone. Customary law is applied to 'natives' particularly in matters of personal law and in the settlement of certain disputes in the local courts; 'non-natives', even if they are living outside the Western Area, are not subject to customary law. A 'non-native' such as a Krio can acquire a leasehold interest in the land only in the provinces. A 'native' can hold and use land without any limitation, including in the Western Area.

56 Non-Citizens (Restriction of Retail Trade) Act, 1965; Non-Citizens (Restriction of Trade and Business) Act, 1965; Non-Citizens (Trade and Business) Act, 1969. A

1966 Act was repealed the same year. See also Alusine Jalloh, *African Entrepreneurship: Muslim Fula Merchants in Sierra Leone*, Ohio University Press, 1999, pp. 85–6.

57 Non-Citizens (Registration, Immigration and Expulsion) Act, 1965.

58 *Akar v. Attorney General*, Sierra Leone Supreme Court, 1967; *Attorney General v. Akar*, Court of Appeal Decision, 1968; *Akar v. Attorney General*, Privy Council Appeal No. 20/68, 30 June 1969. See *African Law Reports Sierra Leone Series 1967–68*; 'John Joseph Akar v. Attorney General', *Journal of African Law*, 12(2) (Summer 1968), pp. 89–109; 'John Joseph Akar v. Attorney General', *Journal of African Law*, 13(2) (Summer 1969), pp. 103–16. Akar was appointed ambassador for Sierra Leone to the United States while the appeal was still pending.

59 Sierra Leone Citizenship Act, No. 4 of 1973.

60 Sierra Leone Citizenship Act, 1973, sections 7 and 8.

61 Act No. 11 of 1983. Although the birth certificate was later amended to require the parents' nationality (rather than race) to be stated, 'Lebanese' may be recorded in cases where the parents are of Lebanese origin, even though the *nationality* of the parents is not Lebanese.

62 'Every person of full age and capacity, neither of whose parents is a person of negro African descent who is resident in Sierra Leone and has been contin-uously so resident for a period of not less than fifteen years may on application being made by him in the manner prescribed, be granted a certificate of naturalization if he satisfies the Minister that he is qualified for naturalization under the provisions set forth in the Third Schedule.' Sierra Leone Citizenship Amendment Act, No. 13 of 1976, amending section 8(3) of the principal Act. The third schedule and section 9 of the Act set out requirements related to a clean criminal record, knowledge of an indigenous Sierra Leonean language, an oath of allegiance, and payment of fees.

63 Sierra Leone Citizenship Act, 1973, section 24.

64 In April 1998, following the restoration of the elected government of President Kabbah, twenty-two people, mostly 'Lebanese', were expelled from Sierra Leone because of their activities during the rebel regime. See Sierra Leone Web News Archive, available at www.sierra-leone.org/slnews0498.html, accessed 5 December 2007.

65 Sierra Leone Citizenship Act, 1976, section 8(5); see also Constitution of Sierra Leone, 1991, Article 76(1).

66 The provisions of the non-discrimination clause in the 1991 constitution are stated not to apply to laws affecting non-citizens, registered or naturalized citizens, and laws limiting rights to citizenship. Constitution of Sierra Leone, 1991, Article 27(4).

67 Based on text and interviews by Umaru Fofana, Freetown, April 2008.

68 Lila's story extracted from Lina Beydoun, 'Lebanese migration to Sierra Leone: issues of transnationalism, gender, citizenship, and the construction of a globalized identity', PhD thesis, Wayne State University, submitted 1 January 2005.

69 Sierra Leone Citizenship (Amendment) Act, No. 11 of 2006.

70 With the exception of an additional right to appeal against the minister's decision in case of deprivation of citizenship by naturalization.

71 Article 20, Investment Promotion Act, 2004.

72 See Immigration and Refugee Board of Canada, Responses to Information Requests, SLE40893.FE, 14 January 2003, www.cisr-irb.gc.ca/en/ research/rir/?action=record. viewrec&gotorec=441394.

73 Among those whose troops became directly involved were Angola, Burundi, Chad, Namibia, Rwanda, Uganda and Zimbabwe.

74 The International Rescue Committee has conducted surveys of 'excess mortality' in DRC since 2000, and estimates that during the period 1998 to 2007 5.4 million excess deaths attributable to the war occurred in DRC, more than two million of them since the formal end of the war in 2002: *Mortality in the Democratic Republic of Congo: An Ongoing Crisis*, International Rescue Committee,

2007. In 2003, the UN Special Rapporteur on the DRC reported 2.7 million displaced persons: *Interim Report of the Special Rapporteur on the Situation of Human Rights in the Democratic Republic of the Congo*, UN Doc. A/58/534, 24 October 2003. The UN High Commissioner for Refugees reported more than 600,000 refugees from DRC in neighbouring countries in 1996, diminishing to 200,000 by 2005: *2005 UNHCR Statistical Yearbook: Dem. Rep. of the Congo*.

75 Population Division of the Department of Economic and Social Affairs, *World Population Prospects: The 2006 Revision*, United Nations, 2007.

76 Except for a couple of years from 1962, when many new provinces were briefly established, there was only one Kivu Province until 1987, when it was split into North and South Kivu and Maniema.

77 Interview with 'Juma', Goma, 10 June 1999, quoted in Stephen Jackson, 'Sons of which soil? The language and politics of autochthony in eastern DR Congo', *African Studies Review*, 49(2), 2006, p. 101.

78 *Ordonnance-loi no.71-020 du 26 mars 1971 rélative à l'acquisition de la nationalité congolaise par les personnes originaires du Rwanda-Urundi établies au Congo au 30 juin 1960*.

79 *Loi no.72-002 du 5 janvier 1972 rélative à la nationalité zairoise*.

80 The 1973 *Loi foncière* –

which is still in force – greatly enhanced state control over land and thus allowed for award of land to favoured individuals for political reasons.

81 Uganda also displaced a large number of Banyarwanda in the early 1980s, including some forty thousand people who claimed Ugandan citizenship and 31,000 people registered with UNHCR as refugees, forcing most of them to seek refuge in Rwanda. See Bonaventure Rutinwa, 'The end of asylum? The changing nature of refugee policies in Africa', *Refugee Survey Quarterly*, 21(1/2), April 2002, p. 6.

82 Le Haut Conseil de la République – Parlement de Transition, *'Résolution sur la nationalité'*, Kinshasa, 28 April 1995, cited in Stephen Jackson, 'Of "doubtful nationality": political manipulation of citizenship in the DR Congo', *Citizenship Studies*, 11(5), November 2007, pp. 481–500. See also 'Briefing on the conflict in South Kivu', IRIN, 10 July 1996.

83 'Operation return the Rwandans to Rwanda'; 'Bukavu and Uvira clean cities': from *Déclaration de la communauté banyamulenge à la conference sur la paix, la sécurité et le développement au Nord et au Sud Kivu*, January 2008.

84 In early 2002, RCD-Goma officer Patrick Mazunzu rejected the rebel movement's authority and took many supporters with him, causing a continuing split in the Banyamulenge community.

RCD-Goma troops tried unsuccessfully to suppress Mazunzu's group. Rwandan government soldiers then joined in attacking the Banyamulenge, a people whose security had once been a pretext for the Rwandan army presence in Congo. See Human Rights Watch, *World Report 2003: Democratic Republic of Congo*, New York, 2003.

85 The discredited colonial-era 'Hamitic hypothesis', in which 'Nilotic' pastoralist invaders were said to have dispossessed Bantu cultivators throughout much of east and central Africa, still has much currency in the discourse of difference today, despite the lack of evidence to support it.

86 Prosecutors in Belgium issued an international arrest warrant for Yerodia in 2000 in connection with these statements, accusing him of breaches of the Geneva Conventions and crimes against humanity (in 2002 the International Court of Justice ruled that Belgium had violated international law in issuing the warrant against a serving minister). See Pieter H. F. Bekker, 'World Court orders Belgium to cancel an arrest warrant issued against the Congolese foreign minister', *ASIL Insights*, February 2002.

87 *Constitution de la Transition*, 5 April 2003, Article 14.

88 After the entry into force in 2002 of the treaty establishing an International Criminal Court, the Kabila government referred the situation in the DRC to the

ICC; several cases are under investigation from Ituri Province, north of the Kivus, in relation to atrocities committed by different ethnic militia (including Tutsi militia) as well as the army, and arrest warrants have been issued. Updates on the investigation into the situation in DRC are available on the website of the International Criminal Court, www.icc-cpi.int/ cases/RDC/s0104/s0104_all.html, accessed 23 November 2007.

89 Stefan Lovgren, '"Gorillas in the Mist" park slashed by squatters', *National Geographic News*, 12 July 2004; Finbarr O'Reilly, 'Mountain gorilla region under threat', *Scotsman*, 23 August 2004; see also information on Virunga National Park at the UN Environment Programme website on the Great Apes Survival Project, at www.unep.org/grasp/Information_ Material/press_rl.asp, accessed 21 July 2008.

90 *'Est Congolais d'origine toute personne appartenant aux groupes ethniques et nationalités dont les personnes et le territoire constituaient ce qui devenu de Congo (présentement la République Démocratique du Congo) à l'indépendance.' Loi n°.04/024 du 12 novembre 2004 rélative a la nationalité congolaise, art. 6.*

91 *Constitution de la République démocratique du Congo, 2006.* The constitution did not, however, repeat the term 'nationalities' from the 2004 law.

92 *Déclaration de la communauté banyamulenge à la* *conference sur la paix, la sécurité et le développement au Nord et au Sud Kivu,* January 2008.

93 'Côte d'Ivoire: what's in a name? A fight for identity', IRIN, 1 November 2005.

94 This outline simplifies the story: among the Burkinabé, many are Mossi from Burkina Faso's central plateau, not one of the Mandé groups; many Mossi are also not Muslim. Among the northern ethnic groups are also the Senoufo, whose members include those who follow Muslim, Christian or traditional religions.

95 Department of Economic and Social Affairs, Population Division, *Trends in Total Migrant Stock: the 2005 Revision*, United Nations, February 2006.

96 Articles 17–23 and 105 of the *Code de la nationalité*, 1961.

97 Articles 25–26 of *Loi no. 61-415 du 14 décembre 1961 portant Code de la nationalité ivoirienne, modifiée par loi no. 72-852 du 21 décembre 1972.*

98 *Loi electoral no. 80-1039, du 1er septembre 1980*, Article 57.

99 *Loi no. 98-750 du 23 décembre 1998 rélative au Domaine foncier rural.*

100 Article 25, Constitution of Côte d'Ivoire, 2000. ('*Le Président de la République ... doit être ivorien d'origine, né de père et mère eux mêmes ivoriens d'origine. Il doit n'avoir jamais renoncé à la nationalité ivoirienne. Il ne doit être jamais prévalu d'une autre nationalité.*')

101 Extracted from: *The New*

Racism: The Political Manipulation of Ethnicity in Côte d'Ivoire, Human Rights Watch, August 2001.

102 Notre Voie, 28 July 2002, cited in Ruth Marshall-Fratani, 'The war of "who is who": autochthony, nationalism and citizenship in the Ivorian crisis', in Sara Dorman, Daniel Hammett and Paul Nugent (eds), Making Nations, Creating Strangers: States and Citizenship in Africa, Brill, 2007.

103 Christian Bouquet, 'La crise ivoirienne par les cartes', Géoconfluences, 4 June 2007, available at geoconfluences. ens-lsh.fr/doc/etpays/Afsubsah/ AfsubsahDoc5.htm, accessed 17 January 2008.

104 Formed by an amalgamation in March 2003 of the MPCI with the Mouvement Populaire Ivoirien du Grand Ouest (MPIGO) and the Mouvement pour la Justice et la Paix (MJP), both based in the south-west.

105 'La présidentielle envisagée par Gbagbo pour fin 2007', L'Humanité, 8 August 2007.

106 Loi no. 2004-412 du 14 août 2004.

107 Loi no. 2004-662 modifiant et complétant la loi 61-415; Loi no. 2004-663 du 17 décembre 2004 portant dispositions spéciales en matière de naturalisation, as implemented by Décision no. 2005-04/PR du 15 juillet 2005. See also Habibou Bangré, 'Côte d'Ivoire: révision du code de la nationalité et de la naturalisation; les amendements apportent des progrès mitigés', 21 December 2004, available at www.afrik. com/article7981.html, accessed 23 November 2007.

108 See Summary of Committee of Ministers meeting 31 May 2006, available at www.cotedivoire-pr.ci/index.php?action=show_page&id_page=388, accessed 29 May 2008.

109 See Statement of the Ministry of Justice and Human Rights on the mobile court process at www.audiencesforaines.gouv.ci/ faq4.php, accessed 29 May 2008; Seventeenth progress report of the Secretary-General on the United Nations Operation in Côte d'Ivoire; UN Security Council Document S/2008/451, 10 July 2008.

110 African soldiers fighting for the French army.

4 Mass denationalization

1 Bonaventure Rutinwa, 'The end of asylum? The changing nature of refugee policies in Africa', Refugee Survey Quarterly, 21(1/2), April 2002, p. 6.

2 Rhoda E. Howard-Hassmann, Human Rights in Commonwealth Africa, Rowman and Littlefield, p. 104.

3 Committee on Economic, Social and Cultural Rights, Consideration of Reports Submitted by States Parties under Articles 16 and 17 of the Covenant: Concluding Observations of the Committee on Economic, Social and Cultural Rights, Nigeria, 13 May 1998, E/C.12/1/Add.23.

4 'Migrants expelled from Gabon', *Migration News*, 2(4), University of California, Davis, March 1995.

5 African Commission on Human and Peoples' Rights (ACHPR), Communication 71/92, *Rencontre Africain pour la Défense des Droits de l'Homme v. Zambia*, (2000); *African Human Rights Law Review* (AHRLR) 321 (ACHPR 1996); Communication 159/96, *Union Interafricaine des Droits de l'Homme and Others v. Angola*, (2000) AHRLR 18 (ACHPR 1997); Communication 249/02, *African Institute for Human Rights and Development in Africa (on behalf of Sierra Leonean refugees in Guinea) v. Republic of Guinea*, (2004) AHRLR 57 (ACHPR 2004).

6 'Operation deports 270,000 foreign citizens', Angola Press Agency, 19 April 2005.

7 'Hundreds march in Niger calling for Arabs expulsion', Reuters, 28 October 2006.

8 Committee on the Elimination of Racial Discrimination, *Consideration of Reports Submitted by States Parties under Article 9 of the Convention: Concluding Observations of the Committee on the Elimination of Racial Discrimination: Libyan Arab Jamahiriya*, CERD/C/64/CO/4, 10 May 2004; Human Rights Watch, *Stemming the Flow: Abuses against Migrants, Asylum Seekers and Refugees in Libya*, September 2006.

9 Report on the African Union Conference of Ministers of Immigration, Ex.CL/197(VII)

28 June–2 July 2005; see also 'African ministers push for protocol on deportation, mass expulsion', PANA, 30 June 2005.

10 This section relies heavily on *The Horn of Africa War: Mass Expulsions and the Nationality Issue (June 1998–April 2002)*, Human Rights Watch, January 2003; many of the notes also come from citations in the original text.

11 'Agreement on Security and Other Related Matters between the Ministries of Internal Affairs of the Governments of Ethiopia and Eritrea', Addis Ababa, 13 May 1994, Article 2.3.

12 Eritrean Nationality Proclamation No. 21/1992, Articles 2–4.

13 Ethiopian Nationality Law, 1930, Article 33(1). The 2003 Proclamation on Ethiopian Nationality removed the gender discrimination, but still prohibits dual nationality.

14 Agreed minutes of the Fourth Ethio-Eritrean Joint High Commission Meeting, 18–19 August 1996, para. 4.3.4.

15 'Government says never to change policy on relations with Eritreans', *Press Digest*, V(25), 18 June 1998, quoting the *Ethiopian Herald* of 13 June 1998.

16 'Eritrea's baseless accusations', Ethiopia Office of Government spokesperson, 9 July 1999.

17 Extracted from *The Horn of Africa War*, p. 3.

18 Proclamation to Provide Foreign Nationals of Ethiopian Origin with Certain Rights to be Exercised in their Country of

Origin (270/2002), 5 February 2002.

19 Maureen Lynch and Katherine Southwick, *Ethiopia-Eritrea: Stalemate Takes Toll on Eritreans and Ethiopians of Eritrean Origin*, Refugees International, 30 May 2008. This report also notes that travel between Eritrea and Ethiopia is prohibited, there is no interstate phone system, and Ethiopians have reportedly been jailed for communicating with friends and relatives in Eritrea via the Internet. At the same time, Ethiopia does accept refugees fleeing political repression and military conscription in Eritrea; a camp on the border housed almost eighteen thousand people as of early 2008.

20 Award of the Eritrea-Ethiopia Claims Commission in *Partial Award (Civilian Claims)*, 44 ILM 601 (2005) at p. 610 (award of 17 December 2004).

21 The nomenclature used for this widely dispersed West African ethnic group (itself made up of several subgroups) is complex: in Commonwealth countries they are usually known as Fula; in countries of the Francophonie as Peul. Pulaar is the language group, and those who speak it are sometimes also known as Halpulaar(en). For a discussion of the issues, see the thread on 'Names for African peoples & language' on the H-Africa log for December 2007, available at www.h-net.org/~africa/, accessed 2 January 2008.

22 Report of the Mission of the Special Rapporteur on Refugees, Asylum Seekers and Internally Displaced Persons in Africa to the Republic of Senegal, African Commission on Human and Peoples' Rights, 2005; David Stone, *Enhancing Livelihood Security among Mauritanian Refugees in Northern Senegal: a Case Study*, UNHCR, June 2005.

23 Human Rights Watch, *Mauritania's Campaign of Terror: State-sponsored Repression of Black Africans*, New York, 1994; see also Human Rights Watch, *World Report* 1989 and 1990.

24 African Commission on Human and Peoples' Rights, Communications 54/91, 61/91, 98/93, 164-196/97 and 210/98, *Malawi African Association and others v. Mauritania*, (2000) AHRLR 149 (ACHPR 2000).

25 See 'Global review of statelessness: Africa', in Maureen Lynch, *Lives on Hold: The Human Cost of Statelessness*, Refugees International, February 2005, p. 29.

26 After their expulsion, most Mauritanians settled along the southern bank of the Senegal river; these settlements are not closed and resemble the surrounding villages, although they usually lack the public services provided to Senegalese villages.

27 Human Rights Committee, 'Concluding observations of the Human Rights Committee: Mali', CCPR/CO/77/MLI, 16 April 2003.

28 'Refugees cautiously optimistic about new initiative',

IRIN, 10 July 2007; Kissy Agyeman, 'Exiled Mauritanians begin tentative retreat back to homeland after 18 years', Global Insight Daily Analysis, 11 July 2007.

29 'Thousands of Mauritanians to return home from Senegal with help of UN Agency', UN News Service, 13 November 2007; 'Is Mauritania ready for its refugees?', IRIN, 16 November 2007.

30 'Briefing paper on the return of expelled Mauritanians to the Islamic Republic of Mauritania following the August 6, 2008 coup', Institute for Human Rights and Development in Africa, October 2008.

5 Internal citizenship

1 For Kenya, see, for example, S. N. Ndegwa, 'Citizenship and ethnicity: an examination of two transition moments in Kenyan politics', *American Political Science Review*, 91(3), 1997, pp. 599–616.

2 During the debates in the constitutional conference that was established in 1953 to decide the form of the future independent state, the British government appointed a commission of inquiry to advise on safeguards for minority rights. This commission, chaired by Henry Willink, reported in 1958. The commission considered each region of Nigeria (Northern, Western and Eastern) and the demands for state creation from minorities. In each case, it rejected the idea of new states on the grounds that: 'it is seldom possible to draw a clean boundary which does not create a fresh minority; the proposed state had in each case become very small by the time it had been pared down to an area in which it was possible to assert with confidence that it was desired'. *Report of the Commission Appointed to Enquire into the Fears of Minorities and the Means of Allaying Them*, Presented to Parliament by the Secretary of State for the Colonies, July 1958, ch. 14, para. 3.

3 These were adopted in 1960, 1963, 1979 and 1999. A 1989 constitution never came into force.

4 'The composition of the Government of the Federation or any of its agencies and the conduct of its affairs shall be carried out in such manner as to reflect the federal character of Nigeria and the need to promote national unity, and also to command national loyalty thereby ensuring that there shall be no predominance of persons from a few States or from a few ethnic or other sectional groups in that government or in any of its agencies.' Constitution of the Federal Republic of Nigeria, 1979, Article 14(3).

5 Constitution of the Federal Republic of Nigeria, 1999, Article 147(3).

6 The closest to a definition is provided in the context of political parties. The 1999 constitution, Article 223(2)(b), provides that the members of the executive of a political party must 'belong to' at least two-thirds of the states of the federation. Article 318(1) in turn

provides that 'belong to', 'when used with reference to a person in a state refers to a person either of whose parents or any of whose grandparents was a member of a community indigenous to that state'.

7 Constitution of the Federal Republic of Nigeria, 1999, Article 42.

8 Human Rights Watch, *'They Do Not Own This Place': Government Discrimination against 'Non-indigenes' in Nigeria*, April 2006, p. 63.

9 Articles 5, 39 and 47 of the Constitution of the Federal Democratic Republic of Ethiopia, 1994, provides: '(3) The right of any Nation, Nationality or People to form its own state is exercisable under the following procedures: When the demand for statehood has been approved by a two-thirds majority of the members of the Council of the Nation, Nationality or People concerned, and the demand is presented in writing to the State Council; When the Council that received the demand has organized a referendum within one year to be held in the Nation, Nationality or People that made the demand; When the demand for statehood is supported by a majority vote in the referendum; When the State Council will have transferred its powers to the Nation, Nationality or People that made the demand; and When the new State created by the referendum without any need for application, directly

becomes a member of the Federal Democratic Republic of Ethiopia.'

10 Constitution of the Federal Republic of Ethiopia, 1994, Preamble and Articles 5 and 39; see also Paul H. Brietzke, 'Ethiopia's "leap in the dark": federalism and self-determination in the new constitution', *Journal of African Law*, 39(1), 1995, pp. 19–38; Jon Abbink, 'Ethnicity and constitutionalism in contemporary Ethiopia', *Journal of African Law*, 41(2), 1997, pp. 159–74; Lahra Smith, 'Voting for an ethnic identity: procedural and institutional responses to ethnic conflict in Ethiopia', *Journal of Modern African Studies*, 45, 2007, pp. 565–94.

6 *The importance of paperwork*

1 UNICEF, *Child Protection Information Sheets*, 2006, p. 13. See also concluding observations of the committee monitoring compliance with the UN Child Rights Convention, available at www. unhchr.ch/tbs/doc.nsf, accessed 3 December 2007.

2 Extracts (lightly edited for spelling and punctuation) from comments posted in 'Is a passport your right?', BBC News Forum discussion, October 2007, available at newsforums.bbc.co.uk/ nol/thread.jspa?forumID=3741& edition=1&ttl=20071028144851, accessed 10 April 2008.

3 Bureau of Democracy, Human Rights, and Labor, 'Swaziland', in *Country Reports on Human Rights Practices 2007*, US Department of State, 11 March 2008.

4 Bureau of Democracy, Human Rights, and Labor, 'Madagascar', in *Country Reports on Human Rights Practices 2007*, US Department of State, 11 March 2008.

5 See, Human Rights Watch, *Struggling through Peace: Return and Resettlement in Angola*, August 2003.

6 UN High Commissioner for Refugees, *Africa Newsletter*, third quarter 2006.

7 Bureau of Democracy, Human Rights, and Labor, *Country Reports on Human Rights Practices 2007*.

8 *Deepak Chamanlal Kamani* v. *Principal Immigration Officer and 2 Others* [2007] eKLR; see also Peter Mwaura, 'Passport is a right for every citizen, not a privilege', *The Nation* (Nairobi), 7 July 2007; Obiora Chinedu Okafor, 'The fundamental right to a passport under Nigerian law: an integrated viewpoint', *Journal of African Law*, 40(1), 1996; *Cuthbert Mambwe Nyirongo* v. *Attorney-General* (1990–1992) ZR 82 (SC).

9 Citizenship and Immigration Control Act, 1999, section 39: 'Every Ugandan shall have the right to a passport or other travel documents.'

10 Committee on the Rights of the Child, Concluding observations: Kenya, CRC/C/KEN/CO/2, 19 June 2007, para. 30; Kenya country report presented at the Second Eastern and Southern Africa Conference on Universal Birth Registration, Mombasa, Kenya, 26–30 September 2005.

11 *An Identity Crisis? Study on the Issuance of National Identity Cards in Kenya*, Kenya National Human Rights Commission, 2007; *The People's Choice: The Report of the Constitution of Kenya Review Commission*, 2002.

12 Children born outside Kenya, however, can under the law obtain citizenship only if their father is a citizen. 1963 Constitution, Article 90.

13 Legal notices No. 264 of 1966 and No. 185 of 1967. The Public Security (Control of Movement) Regulations, L.N.43, 1967.

14 By virtue of this Act the security forces have powers exceeding those of police officers and akin to those that can be used during a declared state of emergency in North-Eastern Province, Isiolo, Marsabit, Meru, Tana River, Lamu district, Samburu, Laikipia and territorial waters.

15 1963 Constitution, Article 81(3)(b). Also excluded are restrictions in the interests of defence, public safety or public order.

16 Preservation of Public Security Act, Laws of Kenya, ch. 57, section 4(2)(b). The Outlying Districts Act and the Special Districts (Administration) Act were repealed by the Statute Law (Repeals and Miscellaneous Amendments) Act, No. 10 of 1997. Although the Preservation of Public Security Act was also amended in 1997 to remove the provisions relating to detention of persons, the other provisions remain in force.

17 In 1984, more than a thousand Kenyan Somalis were killed by security forces in a massacre at Wagalla, North-Eastern Province, for which there has to date been no accountability.

18 Legal Notice No. 5320, *Kenya Government Gazette*, 10 November 1989.

19 Letter from the Office of the President to the District Officer of the Kiunga Division, Lamu, dated 29 July 1992 (on file with CEMIRIDE, the Centre for Minority Rights Development, Nairobi).

20 *Banditry and the Politics of Citizenship: The Case of the Galje'el Somali of Tana River*, MUHURI, 1999.

21 Miscellaneous Civil Application No. 28 of 1999 in Mombasa (on file with CEMIRIDE).

22 Letter from National Registration Bureau, 28 March 2008, cited in Adam Hussein, 'Making of stateless people – the Kenyan style', Open Society Justice Initiative, unpublished, 2008.

23 'Kenya: national registration process leaves minorities on the edge of statelessness', *Bulletin*, Refugees International, 23 May 2008.

24 A summary of the Nubian situation can be found in Maurice Odhiambo Makoloo, *Kenya: Minorities, Indigenous Peoples and Ethnic Diversity*, Minority Rights Group International/CEMIRIDE, 2005.

25 Report of the 1933 Kenya Land Commission, known as the Carter report, quoted in Makoloo,

Kenya: Minorities, Indigenous Peoples and Ethnic Diversity, p. 16.

26 It is claimed that for a long time the Kenyan maps continued to depict Kibera as a forest where nobody lived, and this was what the successive governments continued to claim. All this was in an effort to deny the reality that the Nubians inhabited the area. See, for instance, 'Kibera, the Forgotten City', UN Integrated Regional Information Network (IRIN), 13 September 2006.

27 High Court civil case no. 256 of 2003, Nairobi.

28 Communication 317/106, ACHPR: *The Nubian Community* v. *Kenya*.

29 Summaries of affidavits taken in 2005 by the Open Society Justice Initiative, CEMIRIDE and the Institute for Human Rights and Development in Africa, for the communication brought to the African Commission on Human and Peoples' Rights. Names have been changed.

7 *Excluding candidates*

1 Constitution of the Republic of Zambia, 1991, Article 34(3) (b), added by the Constitution (Amendment) Act No. 18 of 1996. The constitution also provides in Article 7(b) that a person may not be deprived of citizenship except on the grounds that they are the citizen of another country or they have obtained citizenship by fraud.

2 *Zambia Democratic Congress* v. *Attorney General*, Appeal No. 135/96, SCZ Judgment No. 37

of 1999. The Supreme Court of Zambia ultimately (long after the elections had come and gone) ruled against the petition, declaring that the Zambian parliament had the power to adopt the proposed amendment to the constitution without a referendum. The Legal Resources Foundation, a human rights organization, then lodged a complaint against Zambia with the African Commission on Human and Peoples' Rights following the Supreme Court's decision: in 2001 the African Commission ruled that the Zambian government was in violation of several provisions of the African Charter. *Legal Resources Foundation* v. *Zambia* (2001), AHRLR 84 (ACHPR 2001).

3 *Zambia: Elections and Human Rights in the Third Republic*, Human Rights Watch, December 1996.

4 In court, the Zambian government alleged that Banda's father was Malawian; although the trial court found that there was no admissible evidence that Banda was Malawian, it also found that there was insufficient evidence that he was Zambian either. *Amnesty International* v. *Zambia*, African Commission on Human and Peoples' Rights (communication 212/98), (2000) AHRLR 325 (ACHPR 1999), para. 29.

5 *Lewanika and Others* v. *Chiluba*, 1998 ZLR 86. The constitution at the time of independence provided in Article 3(1) as follows: '3(1) Every person who, having

been born in the former protectorate of Northern Rhodesia, is on 23rd October 1964 a British protected person shall become a citizen of Zambia on 24th October 1964.'

6 *Mushota and Another* v. *Kaunda and Another*, 1997/HN/357 unreported. The judgment was published in the *Times of Zambia* on 1 April 1999.

7 *Report of the Electoral Reform Technical Committee (ERTC)*, August 2004, p. 76.

8 *Report of the Constitution Review Commission*, 29 December 2005, pp. 301–4; *Government Reaction to the Electoral Reform Technical Committee Interim Report*, 7 January 2005, p. 14.

9 The government alleged that because Modise was born in the Republic of South Africa and was not a subject of the British Crown at the time of Botswana's independence in 1966, because his father (who had been born in a British protectorate) was not alive in 1966, and because he had not exercised his right to become a naturalized Botswana citizen by October 1968, he could not be considered a citizen of Botswana.

10 See *John K. Modise* v. *Botswana*, Communication No. 97/93, African Commission on Human and Peoples' Rights 14th Annual Activity Report, 2000, reported in (2000) AHRLR 30. The judgment in the decision contradicts itself on facts of the case in paras 5 and 91; what are stated here are believed to be the correct facts.

11 *Modise* v. *Botswana*, African Commission on Human and Peoples' Rights, para. 96.

12 In 2004 the government reportedly offered Modise 100,000 pula (around US$21,000 at the contemporary exchange rate) as compensation for his 1978 deportation from Botswana in response to the African Commission's ruling, an offer he is said to have rejected. See Donny Dithato, 'State in secret talks with Modise', *Mmegi*, 25 August.

13 *Bhekindlela Thomas Ngwenya* v. *The Deputy Prime Minister*, 1970–76 SLR (HC) 88.

14 Immigration (Amendment) Act No. 22 of 1972.

15 *Bhekindlela Thomas Ngwenya* v. *The Deputy Prime Minister and the Chief Immigration Officer*, 1970–76 SLR (HC) 119.

16 *Bhekindlela Thomas Ngwenya* v. *The Deputy Prime Minister and the Chief Immigration Officer*, 1970–76 SLR (CA) 123.

17 See also Maseko Thulani Rudolf, 'The writing of a democratic constitution in Africa with reference to Swaziland and Uganda', LLM thesis, University of Pretoria, 2005.

18 Citizenship Order, King's Order in Council, 22 of 1974, 3 September 1974, *Swaziland Government Gazette*, 1974, cited in Hugh Macmillan, 'A nation divided? The Swazi in Swaziland and the Transvaal, 1865–1986', in Leroy Vail (ed.), *The Creation of Tribalism in Southern Africa*, James Currey, 1989.

19 See International Labour Organization, Committee on Freedom of Association, Swaziland (Case No. 1884), 23 May 1996, Report No. 306 (vol. LXXX, 1997, series B, No. 1).

20 'Enforcement of Immigration Act intensifies', *The Times of Swaziland*, 24 April 2003; *Legalbrief Africa*, issue No. 024, 21 April 2003. The Swaziland Citizenship Act 1992, the relevant legislation at the time and still in force, provides that those who have citizenship by registration may be deprived of it if they subsequently acquire another citizenship, but makes no other provisions on dual nationality. The 2005 constitution that has since come into force does not change this position. See also *Swaziland: Law, Custom and Politics: Constitutional Crisis and the Breakdown in the Rule of Law*, International Bar Association Human Rights Institute, March 2003; *Fact-finding Mission to the Kingdom of Swaziland*, Report of the Centre for the Independence of Judges and Lawyers, International Commission of Jurists, 10 June 2003; *Swaziland: Human Rights at Risk*, AI Index: AFR 55/004/2004, Amnesty International, July 2004.

21 'A person who has Khontaed, that is to say, has been accepted as a Swazi in accordance with customary law and in respect of whom certificate of Khonta granted by or at the direction of the King is in force, shall be a citizen of Swaziland.' Swaziland

Citizenship Act No. 14 of 1992, section 5. See also Constitution of Swaziland, 2005, Article 42, which provides that persons born before the constitution came into effect are citizens 'by operation of law' if either parent is a citizen and also if the person is 'generally regarded as Swazi by descent'. Article 43 of the constitution removes this (not entirely clear) ethnic basis for children born after the constitution came into effect, but entrenches gender discrimination, providing that citizenship is only passed by a father who is a Swazi citizen.

22 'Tanzania drops envoy to Nigeria over citizenship', *Guardian*, Dar es Salaam, 5 February 2001.

23 'Veteran editor stripped of citizenship', *Guardian,* Dar es Salaam, 8 August 2006; Ernest Mpinganjira, 'Intimidation of media exposes Tanzania's fear of criticism', *Sunday Standard*, 13 August 2006.

24 Zambia Immigration and Deportation Act, Laws of Zambia, ch. 123, section 26(2): 'Any person who in the opinion of the Minister is by his presence or his conduct likely to be a danger to peace or good order in Zambia may be deported from Zambia pursuant to a warrant under the hand of the Minister.'

25 *Jackson* v. *Attorney General* (1979) Z.R. 167; *Walulya* v. *Attorney General* (1984) Z.R 89.

26 *Vijay Giri Anand Giri Goswami* v. *Attorney General* (HP/3671), 1994.

27 *Roy Clarke* v. *The Attorney General* (HP/003), 2004.

28 *Attorney General* v. *Roy Clarke*, SCZ Appeal No. 96A/2004, 24 January 2008.

29 Under section 7 of the Immigration Act, the categories of prohibited immigrants are: (a) people who are likely to become a public charge 'by reason of infirmity of mind or body' or because of insufficient means of support; (b) people who are 'idiot or epileptic', 'insane or mentally deficient', 'deaf and dumb, or deaf and blind, or dumb and blind'; (c) people who are infected by a proscribed disease; (d) people who are or ever have been a prostitute or involved with prostitution; (e) people who have either been sentenced in Botswana or elsewhere for an offence which 'if committed in Botswana, would be punishable with imprisonment without the option of a fine'; (f) anyone considered by the president to be an 'undesirable inhabitant'; and (g) the wife and minor children of the prohibited immigrant. See Botswana Immigration Act, Laws of Botswana, ch. 25:02, section 7. While section 11 allows for an appeal process for people who want to challenge their designation as a prohibited immigrant, no appeal is allowed for people who under section 7(f) have been declared a prohibited immigrant by the president. Moreover, 11(6) states that 'no court shall question the adequacy of the grounds for any such declaration'.

30 *Kenneth Good* v. *The Attorney General* (Civil Appeal No. 28 of 2005), 27 July 2005.

8 *Naturalization and integration*

1 Department of Home Affairs, *Annual Report 2006–2007*, Government of South Africa, 2008, p. 47.

2 'Accès à la nationalité sénégalaise: les mêmes textes pour tous les demandeurs', *APA News*, 13 August 2007.

3 'About 6000 foreigners may become Swazi citizens', *The Times of Swaziland*, 17 August 2005.

4 'Over 30,000 granted citizenship', *Daily News*, Gaborone, 31 March 2005.

5 United Nations Secretary-General, *Assistance to refugees, returnees and displaced persons in Africa*, report to the General Assembly, A/61/301, 29 August 2006.

6 Mulki Al-Sharmani, 'Livelihood and identity constructions of Somali refugees in Cairo', *Forced Migration and Refugee Studies Working Paper No. 2*, American University in Cairo, July 2003, p. 6.

7 Extracted from, Oroub El-Abed, 'Deportation from Cairo', 5 March 2004, available at www.achr.nu/newen35.htm.

8 Law No. 154 of 2004 amending some provisions of Law No. 26 of 1975 concerning Egyptian nationality, *Official Gazette*, vol. 28, 14 July 2004. See also www.learningpartnership.org/citizenship/category/countries/egypt, accessed 13 November 2007.

9 For further details see *Citizenship Law in Africa: A Comparative Study*, Open Society Institute, 2009.

10 Story contributed by Khoti Kamanga.

11 A discussion of these amnesties can be found in Bronwyn Harris, 'A Foreign experience: violence, crime and xenophobia during South Africa's transition', *Violence and Transition Series*, vol. 5, Centre for the Study of Violence and Reconciliation, South Africa, August 2001.

12 See essays in Jonathan Crush and Vincent Williams (eds), *The New South Africans? Immigration Amnesties and Their Aftermath*, Idasa, Cape Town, 1999; Human Rights Watch, *Prohibited Persons: Abuse of Undocumented Migrants, Asylum Seekers and Refugees in South Africa*, New York, March 1998.

13 South Africa Refugees Act (No. 130 of 1998), entry into force 2000; South Africa Immigration Act (No. 13 of 2002), entry into force 2003.

14 As of 2005, around thirty thousand people were recognized as refugees in South Africa, with more than a further 140,000 who had applied for asylum. UN High Commissioner for Refugees, *Statistical Yearbook 2005*; more than fifty thousand additional applications were made in 2006 and more than forty-five thousand in 2007, while the top five countries of origin in 2007 were Zimbabwe, DRC, Ethiopia, Malawi

and Somalia. 'South Africa gets 45,673 asylum seekers in 2007, warns of rising numbers', UNHCR press statement, 26 February 2008; Florencia Belvedere et al., *National Refugee Baseline Survey: Final Report*, Community Agency for Social Enquiry (CASE), Johannesburg, 2003, p. 6.

15 The Supreme Court of Appeal ruled in the 2003 *Watchenuka* case that asylum seekers were entitled to work and study while awaiting the determination of their applications. The Constitutional Court in the *Khosa* case upheld the right of permanent residents to receive social security. In the case of *S* v. *Manuel*, the High Court held that the right to legal aid that is recognized in section 35(3)(g) of the constitution applies to foreigners without correct immigration papers who are accused in a South African court. *Minister of Home Affairs and Others* v. *Watchenuka and Another*, 2004(4) SA 326(SCA); *Khosa and Others* v. *Minister of Social Development and Others; Mahlaule and Another* v. *Minister of Social Development and Others*, 2004(6) SA 505(CC); *S* v. *Manuel* 2001(4) SA 1351(W). See also *Larbi-Odam and Others* v. *Member of the Executive Council for Education (North-West Province) and Another*, 1998 (1) SA 745 (CC).

16 See, for example, *Citizenship, Violence and Xenophobia in South Africa: Perceptions from South African Communities*, Human Sciences Research Council, Pretoria, June 2008. South African men in particular found the presence of the newcomers threatening.

17 The Frente Popular para la Liberación de Saguia el-Hamra y de Río de Oro (Frente POLISARIO), named after the two former Spanish provinces making up the territory.

18 UN High Commissioner for Refugees, *Statistical Yearbook 2005*.

19 Pablo San Martin, 'Nationalism, identity and citizenship in the Western Sahara', *Journal of North African Studies*, 10(3/4), September–December 2005; Human Rights Watch, *Human Rights in Western Sahara and in the Tindouf Refugee Camps*, December 2008; telephone interview with Francesco Bastagli, former Special Representative of the UN Secretary-General for Western Sahara, May 2008.

20 See the website of the UN Mission for a Referendum in Western Sahara (MINURSO), available at www.un.org/Depts/dpko/missions/minurso, accessed 3 December 2007. The 'Settlement Plan', based on a framework initially proposed by the OAU in 1983, was originally put forward by the UN and agreed to in principle by the parties in 1988. It was ultimately approved by UN Security Council Resolution 690 of 29 April 1991. For background and updates on the peace negotiations, see Issaka K. Souaré, 'Western Sahara: is there light at the end of the tunnel?', *ISS Paper 155*, Institute

of Security Studies, South Africa, November 2007.

21 San Martin, 'Nationalism, identity and citizenship in the Western Sahara', footnotes 7 and 47; Human Rights Watch, *Human Rights in Western Sahara and in the Tindouf Refugee Camps*, December 2008, p. 23.

22 For background, see Dr Sidi Omar, 'The right to self-determination and the indigenous people of Western Sahara', *Cambridge Review of International Affairs*, 21(1), March 2008.

23 A well-referenced list is maintained on Wikipedia at: en.wikipedia.org/wiki/Legal_status_of_Western_Sahara, accessed 13 June 2008.

24 This position was confirmed in a 2002 opinion by the UN Legal Counsel, which recalled that Spanish Sahara was included in 1963 in the list of non-self-governing territories under Chapter XI of the UN Charter, and that the transfer of administrative authority over the territory to Morocco and Mauritania in 1975 did not transfer sovereignty nor affect the international status of Western Sahara as a non-self-governing territory. Letter dated 29 January 2002 from the Under-Secretary-General for Legal Affairs, the Legal Counsel, addressed to the president of the Security Council, UN Document S/2002/161.

25 In 2007, the Spanish Supreme Court ruled in favour of a Sahrawi refugee who had applied to be recognized as stateless by the Spanish authorities, even though she had travelled to Spain on an Algerian passport granted to enable her to seek medical treatment seven years earlier. Case of Ms Khadijatou Bourkari Dafa, Recurso Casacion Num: 10503/2003.

26 Decree 2258 of 10 August 1976.

27 *Code de la nationalité marocaine*, ch. IV.

28 In 1998, the Moroccan Supreme Court declared itself unable to rule on the nationality of Abraham Serfaty, who, though not a Sahrawi, had spent seventeen years in prison for advocating self-determination for Western Sahara, from 1974 to 1991, and after his release was expelled from the country on the grounds that he was not Moroccan. Serfaty, who is Jewish, was born in Morocco, worked for years as a high-ranking civil servant and lived there until his expulsion. He was not given the opportunity to challenge the expulsion in court before he was forced into exile. He was, however, eventually allowed to return to Morocco. *Morocco/Western Sahara: 'Turning the Page': Achievements and Obstacles*, Amnesty International, 4 August 1999, Index Number: MDE 29/001/1999, and annual report sections on Morocco/Western Sahara.

29 *Morocco/Western Sahara: Stop the Judicial Harassment of Sahrawi Human Rights Defenders*, Amnesty International, 5 February 2007, Index Number: MDE 29/003/2007.

30 Human Rights Watch, *Letter to King Mohammed VI on the Trial of Sahrawi Human Rights Defenders in the Western Sahara*, 8 December 2005.

9 *Last words*

1 OAU Assembly, Res. 16 (II), Cairo Summit, 2nd Ordinary Session, 1964.

2 'Symposium on the African Union: Statement of Consensus', African Development Forum III: Defining Priorities for Regional Integration, Addis Ababa, Ethiopia, 3 March 2002.

3 Strategic Plan of the Commission of the African Union, 2004–2007; Report of the First Conference of Intellectuals of Africa and the Diaspora, Dakar, Senegal, 6–9 October 2004; Report on the African Union Conference of Ministers of Immigration to the African Union Executive Council Seventh Ordinary Session 28 June–2 July 2005, EX.CL/197 (VII).

4 At subregional level freedom of movement has made greater progress. The Economic Community of West African States has had a subregional passport and internal freedom of movement since 1979, as well as rules intended to make it easier to establish businesses across the regional borders. The revived East African Community has created a free-movement regime among the five countries that constitute it, with a common internal passport. Within the Southern African Development Community, however, disagreements over the content of a protocol on free movement led to a much watered-down version being adopted by the SADC summit in 2005, which provided very few additional rights to those already held. Other regional communities are further behind.

Further reading

General

Appiah, Kwame Anthony (1992) *In My Father's House: Africa in the Philosophy of Culture*, Oxford: Oxford University Press.

Coquery-Vidrovitch, Catherine (2001) 'Nationalité et citoyenneté en Afrique occidentale français: originaires et citoyens dans le Sénégal colonial', *Journal of African History*, 42(2): 285–305.

Dorman, Sara, Daniel Hammett and Paul Nugent (eds) (2007) *Making Nations, Creating Strangers: States and Citizenship in Africa*, Leiden: Brill.

Geschiere, Peter and Stephen Jackson (2006) 'Autochthony and the Crisis of Citizenship: Democratization, Decentralization, and the Politics of Belonging', *African Studies Review* (Special Issue: Autochthony and the Crisis of Citizenship), 49(2): 1–7.

Herbst, Jeffrey (1999) 'The role of citizenship laws in multiethnic societies: evidence from Africa', in Richard Joseph (ed.), *State, Conflict and Democracy in Africa*, Boulder, CO: Lynne Rienner.

— (2000) *States and Power in Africa: Comparative Lessons in Authority and Control*, Princeton, NJ: Princeton University Press, ch. 8: 'The politics of migration and citizenship'.

Howard-Hassmann, Rhoda E. (1986) *Human Rights in Commonwealth Africa*, Lanham, MD: Rowman and Littlefield, ch. 5: 'State formation and communal rights'.

Mamdani, Mahmood (1996) *Citizen and Subject: Contemporary Africa and the Legacy of Late Colonialism*, Princeton, NJ: Princeton University Press.

— (2001) 'Beyond settler and native as political identities: overcoming the political legacy of colonialism', *Comparative Studies in Society and History*, 4(4): 651–64.

Nyamnjoh, Francis B. (2007) 'From bounded to flexible citizenship: lessons from Africa', *Citizenship Studies*, 11(1): 73–82.

Nzongola-Ntalaja, Georges (2004) 'Citizenship, political violence, and democratization in Africa', *Global Governance*, 10(4): 403–7.

Peil, Margaret (1971) 'The expulsion of West African aliens', *Journal of Modern African Studies*, 9(2): 203–29.

Ranger, Terence (1983) 'The invention of tradition in colonial Africa', in Eric Hobsbawm and Terence Ranger (eds), *The*

Invention of Tradition, Cambridge: Cambridge University Press.

Roitman, Janet (2007) 'The right to tax: economic citizenship in the Chad Basin', *Citizenship Studies*, 11(2): 187–209.

Rutinwa, Bonaventure (2002) 'The end of asylum? The changing nature of refugee policies in Africa', *Refugee Survey Quarterly*, 2(1/2): 12–41.

Weil, Patrick (2003) *Le statut des musulmans en Algérie coloniale: une nationalité française dénaturée*, EUI Working Paper, HEC No. 2003/3, European University Institute.

Whitaker, Beth Elise (2005) 'Citizens and foreigners: democratization and the politics of exclusion in Africa', *African Studies Review*, 48(1): 109–26.

Young, Crawford (2002) 'Nationalism and ethnicity in Africa', *Review of Asian and Pacific Studies*, 28: 1–19.

Banyarwanda in Rwanda, DRC, Tanzania

Gasarasi, Charles P. (1990) 'The Mass naturalization and further integration of Rwandese refugees in Tanzania: process, problems and prospects', *Journal of Refugee Studies*, 3(2): 88–109.

Human Rights Watch (1996) *Forced to Flee: Violence against the Tutsis in Zaire*, July.

— (1997) *Zaire: 'Attacked by All Sides'*, March.

— (1997) *Zaire: Transition, War and Human Rights*, April.

— (1997) *What Kabila is Hiding: Civilian Killings and Impunity in Congo*, October.

— (1997) *Transition and Human Rights Violations in Congo*, December.

— (1999) *Leave None to Tell the Story: Genocide in Rwanda*.

— (2004) *DR Congo: War Crimes in Bukavu*, June.

— (2007) *Renewed Crisis in North Kivu*, October.

Jackson, Stephen (2006) 'Sons of which soil? The language and politics of autochthony in eastern DR Congo', *African Studies Review*, 49(2): 95–123.

— (2007) 'Of "doubtful nationality": political manipulation of citizenship in the DR Congo', *Citizenship Studies*, 11(5): 481–500.

Mararo, Stanislas Bucyalimwe (2000) 'La guerre des chiffres: une constante dans la politique au Nord-Kivu', *L'Afrique des Grands Lacs Annuaire 1999–2000*.

— (2002) 'Le Nord-Kivu au coeur de la crise congolaise', *L'Afrique des Grands Lacs Annuaire 2001–2002*.

Nzongola-Ntalaja, Georges (2002) *The Congo from Leopold to Kabila: A People's History*, London: Zed Books.

Report on the Situation of Human Rights in Zaire by the Special Rapporteur, Mr Robert Garretón, in accordance with Commission resolution 1996/77, UN Doc. E/CN.4/1997/6/Add.1.

Reyntjens, Filip (1985) *Pouvoir*

et droit au Rwanda, Tervuren: Musée Royal de l'Afrique Central.

Van Acker, Frank (1999) 'La "Pembenisation" du Haut-Kivu: opportunisme et droits fonciers revisités', in *L'Afrique des Grands Lacs Annuaire 1998–1999*.

Vlassenroot, Koen (2002) 'Citizenship, identity formation & conflict in South Kivu: the case of the Banyamulenge', *Review of African Political Economy*, 29(93/94): 499–515.

Côte d'Ivoire

Banégas, Richard and Ruth Marshall-Fratani (2007) 'Côte d'Ivoire: negotiating identity and citizenship', in Morten Bøås and Kevin C. Dunn (eds), *African Guerrillas: Raging against the Machine*, Boulder, CO: Lynne Rienner, pp. 81–111.

Dozon, Jean-Pierre (1997) 'L'étranger et l'allochtone en Côte d'Ivoire', in B. Contamin et H. Memel-Fotê (eds), *Le modèle ivoirien en question: crise, réajustements, récompositions*, Paris: Karthala, pp. 779–98.

Human Rights Watch (2001) *The New Racism: The Political Manipulation of Ethnicity in Côte d'Ivoire*, August.

International Crisis Group (2003) '*The War is Not Yet Over*', Africa Report 72, 28 November.

— (2004) *No Peace in Sight*, Africa Report 82, 12 July.

— (2005) *The Worst May be Yet to Come*, Africa Report 90, 24 March.

— (2006) *Peace as an Option*, Africa Report 109, 17 May.

— (2007) *Can the Ouagadougou Agreement Bring Peace?*, Africa Report 127, 27 June.

— (2008) *Ensuring Credible Elections*, Africa Report 139, 22 April.

Langer, Arnim (2005) 'Horizontal inequalities and violent conflict: Côte d'Ivoire Country Paper', Occasional Paper 2005/32, UNDP Human Development Report Office.

Marshall-Fratani, Ruth (2007) 'The war of "who is who": autochthony, nationalism and citizenship in the Ivorian crisis', in Sara Dorman, Daniel Hammett and Paul Nugent (eds), *Making Nations, Creating Strangers: States and Citizenship in Africa*, Leiden: Brill.

Politique Africaine (June 2000) Special edition: *Côte d'Ivoire, la tentation ethnonationaliste*, 78.

Toungara, Jeanne Maddox (2001) 'Ethnicity and political crisis in Côte d'Ivoire', *Journal of Democracy*, 12(3): 63–72.

Weiss, Pierre (2004) 'L'Opération Licorne en Côte d'Ivoire: banc d'essai de la nouvelle politique française de sécurité en Afrique', *Annuaire français de relations internationales*, V.

Zoro Bi, Epiphane (2004) *Juge en Côte d'Ivoire*, Paris: Karthala.

Ethiopia

Abbink, Jon (1997) 'Ethnicity and constitutionalism in contemporary Ethiopia', *Journal of African Law*, 41(2): 159–74.

Brietzke, Paul H. (1995) 'Ethiopia's "leap in the dark": federalism and self-determination in the new constitution', *Journal of African Law*, 39(1): 19–38.

Human Rights Watch (2003) *The Horn of Africa War: Mass Expulsions and the Nationality Issue (June 1998–April 2002)*, January.

Smith, Lahra (2007) 'Voting for an ethnic identity: procedural and institutional responses to ethnic conflict in Ethiopia', *Journal of Modern African Studies*, 45(4): 565–94.

Kenya and Uganda

Barya, John Jean (2000) 'Reconstituting Ugandan citizenship under the 1995 constitution: a conflict of nationalism, chauvinism and ethnicity', *CBR Working Paper No. 55*, Kampala: Centre for Basic Research.

Makoloo, Maurice Odhiambo (2005) *Kenya: Minorities, Indigenous Peoples and Ethnic Diversity*, Minority Rights Group International/Cemiride.

Nanjira, Daniel D. C. Don (1976) *The Status of Aliens in East Africa: Asians and Europeans in Tanzania, Uganda and Kenya*, New York: Praeger.

Sharma, Vishnu D. and F. Wooldridge (1974) 'Some legal questions arising from the expulsion of the Ugandan Asians', *International and Comparative Law Quarterly*, 23(2): 397–425.

Smith, Alan H. (1971) 'Prevention of discrimination under Kenya law', *International and Comparative Law Quarterly*, 20(1): 136–42.

Mauritania

Human Rights Watch (1994) *Mauritania's Campaign of Terror: State-sponsored Repression of Black Africans*.

Stone, David (2005) *Enhancing Livelihood Security among Mauritanian Refugees in Northern Senegal: A case study*, UNHCR.

Nigeria

Adepoju, Aderanti (1984) 'Illegals and expulsion in Africa: the Nigerian experience', *International Migration Review*, 18(3), special issue: *Irregular Migration: An International Perspective*, pp. 426–36.

Aluko, Olajide (1985) 'The expulsion of illegal aliens from Nigeria: a study in Nigeria's decision making', *African Affairs*, 84(337): 539–60.

Human Rights Watch (2006) *'They Do Not Own This Place': Government Discrimination against 'Non-indigenes' in Nigeria*, April.

The 'Lebanese' in Sierra Leone and west Africa

Akyeampong, Emmanuel K. (2006) 'Race, identity and citizenship in black Africa: the case of the Lebanese in Ghana', *Africa*, 76(3): 297–323.

Bierwirth, Chris (1999) 'The Lebanese communities of Côte d'Ivoire', *African Affairs*, 98: 79–99.

Beydoun, Lina (2005) 'Lebanese migration to Sierra Leone: issues of transnationalism, gender, citizenship, and the construction of a globalized identity', Unpublished PhD thesis, Wayne State University.

Jalloh, Alusine (1999) *African Entrepreneurship: Muslim Fula Merchants in Sierra Leone*, Athens: Ohio University Press.

Van der Laan, H. L. (1975) *The Lebanese Traders in Sierra Leone: Change and Continuity in Africa*, The Hague: Mouton.

South and southern Africa

Crush, Jonathan and Vincent Williams (eds) (1999) *The New South Africans? Immigration Amnesties and their Aftermath*, Cape Town: Idasa.

Human Rights Watch (1998) *Prohibited Persons: Abuse of Undocumented Migrants, Asylum Seekers and Refugees in South Africa*.

Human Sciences Research Council (2008) *Citizenship, Violence and Xenophobia in South Africa: Perceptions from South African Communities*, Pretoria.

Klaaren, Jonathan (1999) 'Post-apartheid citizenship in South Africa', available at www.law.wits.ac.za/school/klaaren/klaarenc.htm, accessed 6 November 2007.

Klaaren, Jonathan and Bonaven-ture Rutinwa (2004) 'Towards the harmonisation of im-migration and refugee law in SADC', Migration Dialogue for Southern Africa (MIDSA), Report no. 1.

Landau, Loren B. (2004) 'The laws of (in)hospitality: black Africans in South Africa', Forced Migration Working Paper Series no. 7, University of the Witwatersrand.

Minaar, Anthony and Mike Hough (1996) *Who Goes There? Perspectives on Clandestine Migration and Illegal Aliens in Southern Africa*, Pretoria: HSRC Publishers.

Nyamnjoh, Francis B. (2006) *Insiders and Outsiders: Citizenship and Xenophobia in Contemporary Southern Africa*, London: Codesria/Zed Books.

Oucho, John O. and Jonathan Crush (2001) 'Contra free movement: South Africa and the SADC migration protocols', *Africa Today*, 8(3): 139–58.

Vail, Leroy (ed.) (1989) *The Creation of Tribalism in Southern Africa*, London: James Currey.

Western Sahara

Hodges, Tony (1983) *Western Sahara: The Roots of a Desert War*, New York: Lawrence Hill & Co.

Human Rights Watch (2008) *Human Rights in Western Sahara and in the Tindouf Refugee Camps*.

Omar, Sidi M. (2008) 'The right to self-determination and the indigenous people of Western Sahara', *Cambridge Review of International Affairs*, 21(1): 41–57.

San Martin, Pablo (2005) 'Nationalism, identity and citizenship in the Western Sahara', *Journal of North African Studies*, 10(3/4): 565–92.

Zimbabwe

Hammar, Amanda, Brian Raftopoulos and Stig Jensen (2003) *Zimbabwe's Unfinished Business: Rethinking Land, State and Nation in the Context of Crisis*, Harare: Weaver Press.

Moyo, Sam, Blair Rutherford and Dede Amanor-Wilks (2000) 'Land reform and changing social relations for farm workers in Zimbabwe', *Review of African Political Economy*, 27(84): 181–202.

Nkiwane, Tandeka C. (2000) 'Gender, citizenship, and constitutionalism in Zimbabwe: the fight against Amendment 14', *Citizenship Studies*, 4(3): 325–38.

Raftopoulos, Brian (2007) 'Nation, race and history in Zimbabwe', in Sara Dorman, Daniel Hammett and Paul Nugent (eds), *Making Nations, Creating Strangers: States and Citizenship in Africa*, Leiden: Brill.

Rutherford, Blair (2007) 'Shifting grounds in Zimbabwe: citizenship and farm workers in the new politics of land', in Sara Dorman, Daniel Hammett and Paul Nugent (eds), *Making Nations, Creating Strangers: States and Citizenship in Africa*, Leiden: Brill.

Selby, Angus (2006) 'Commercial farmers and the state: interest group politics and land reform in Zimbabwe', Unpublished DPhil thesis, Oxford University.

Index